L. G. Wright Glass

The West Virginia Museum of American Glass, Ltd.

L. G. Wright book project editorial committee:

Neila Bredehoft
Helen Jones
Dean Six

4880 Lower Valley Road, Atglen, PA 19310 USA

Copyright © 2003 by The West Virginia Museum of American Glass, Ltd.
Library of Congress Control Number: 2003103152

All rights reserved. No part of this work may be reproduced or used in any form or by any means—graphic, electronic, or mechanical, including photocopying or information storage and retrieval systems—without written permission from the publisher.

The scanning, uploading and distribution of this book or any part thereof via the Internet or via any other means without the permission of the publisher is illegal and punishable by law. Please purchase only authorized editions and do not participate in or encourage the electronic piracy of copyrighted materials.

"Schiffer," "Schiffer Publishing Ltd. & Design," and the "Design of pen and ink well" are registered trademarks of Schiffer Publishing Ltd.

Designed by Mark David Bowyer
Type set in Americana XBd BT/Aldine 721 BT

ISBN: 0-7643-1861-6
Printed in China
1 2 3 4

Published by Schiffer Publishing Ltd.
4880 Lower Valley Road
Atglen, PA 19310
Phone: (610) 593-1777; Fax: (610) 593-2002
E-mail: Info@schifferbooks.com
Please visit our web site catalog at **www.schifferbooks.com**
We are always looking for people to write books on new and related subjects. If you have an idea for a book please contact us at the above address.

This book may be purchased from the publisher.
Include $3.95 for shipping.
Please try your bookstore first.
You may write for a free catalog.

In Europe, Schiffer books are distributed by
Bushwood Books
6 Marksbury Ave.
Kew Gardens
Surrey TW9 4JF England
Phone: 44 (0)20-8392-8585
Fax: 44 (0)20-8392-9876
E-mail: Bushwd@aol.com
Free postage in the UK. Europe: air mail at cost

Contents

Introduction 4
   Pricing & How The Book Is Organized 4
   History 5
   Who Made the Glass L. G. Wright sold? 24
L. G. Wright and Early American
   Pattern Glass Goblets 28
L. G. Wright Glass Co Mold Disposition 30
L. G. Wright Catalog Illustrations 35
Index 191

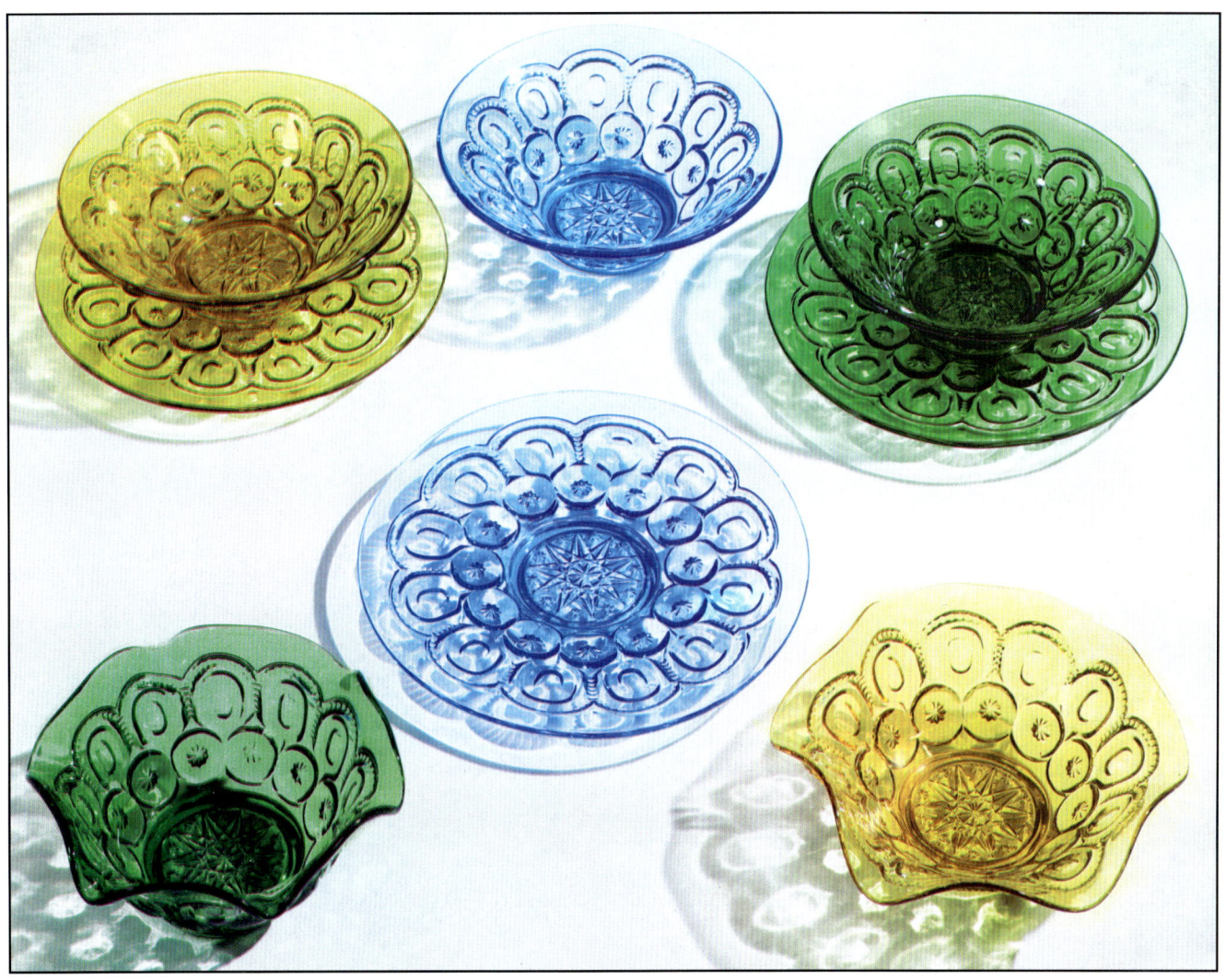

Introduction

This book came into existence through a fortunate occurrence: the West Virginia Museum of American Glass, Ltd. (WVMAG), a not-for-profit museum interested in all American glass, acquired a large portion of the company records of the L. G. Wright Glass Co. This acquisition came about at the last in a series of public auctions of the assets of the L. G. Wright Glass Company. WVMAG's actual purchases were many over the four-day auction, held late summer 1999 at the Wright Company site in New Martinsville, West Virginia.

When the Museum cataloged the purchased material, we realized there was a great deal of information, literally boxes and boxes of information, that tell an important story. It is also a complex story. Not all of the Wright story is told in the material we acquired. Others may tell the same story in a different way and at least one previous book presents some of this same information and tells one possible version of the story. But the West Virginia Museum of American Glass (WVMAG), a relatively young and small museum, has an outstanding reputation for sharing its assets and information. Indeed that dissemination of glass history is a part of the corporate charter. While WVMAG is dedicated to all American glass, and comparing and contrasting those various stories, it is strongest on West Virginia stories, those closest to home. And Wright was and is a West Virginia story.

Thus, given the significant volume of Wright material, a book project seemed the best possible way to spread the information as widely as possible. You hold in your hands the result of that project. WVMAG hopes to add future glass titles to its efforts at sharing the collection it is building. Presently WVMAG publishes a series of glass catalog reprints and monographs on lesser-known glass topics to aid in the mission of information sharing. Learn more about WVMAG at the back of this book. And enjoy.

Pricing & How the Book is Organized

The West Virginia Museum of American Glass, Ltd., as a not for profit organization with certain ethical obligations as a public museum, is not and should not be in the business of determining values for glass.

This book was edited by a committee, and the prices were established in the same manner. Let us explain. A minimum of three people and as many as eight people looked at every image used and offered pricing suggestions. Often the discrepancies for values suggested were as little as five or ten dollars, frequently several people suggested the exact numbers. The number of times this agreement happened was almost frightening. Agreement within a committee is rare. When it occurs and reoccurs, it seems fated. When any discrepancy in value was more than a few dollars, an average was determined or explanations were given that led to a consensus. All prices in this book were agreed upon by a group and were agreed upon with complete consensus. There were no exceptions.

The "group" was a selection of four dealers, four collectors, and two nationally recognized Early American Pattern Glass collector-researchers. While not everyone felt qualified to express an opinion on every object or type of glass, each volunteer participated where they felt comfortable. We frequently worked in groups, traveling several states to be together and forge the pricing document. Sharing photocopies of the images and then passing documents via e-mail when needed allowed us to arrive at electronic consensus. No one participating in the pricing has any vested interest in selling their collection or profiteering from the prices and information contained in this book.

No one can suggest perfect pricing. And the indications of value in this book are only that: *Suggestions Of Possible Value*. Regional differences, concentrations of collectors for specific types of glass, and other elements make prices higher and lower under diverse circumstances. Use your judgment. The numbers suggested are only that: suggestions. Pieces will be found offered for sale (and selling) for much more than we suggest. Pieces will also be found at far less than the prices suggested. Use your judgment.

When you hold this book and consider the prices contained herein, only one thing is certain: a number of good people volunteered their time to work many hours creating what they believe is a fair and realistic set of reasonable suggested values for the objects shown. It is to be used and viewed accordingly.

The story of Wright Glass is told here by original documents as much as possible. The attempt was to provide a minimum of our interpretation and let the archives do the storytelling. All of the illustrations that constitute the body of the book are the original company photos used as illustrations by the traveling salesmen or are from company catalogs.

The captions for the catalog pages all use the original Wright pattern names and line or piece numbers. For the few occasions where we believed confusion was possible due to a lack of name or some other ascertainable reference, we have created a few names for objects or patterns. These, and they are uncommon, are set for in "quotations" to denote that they are not original to Wright.

History

West Virginia has long been one of the centers of American glass production. When America moved west at the beginning of the 1800s, the need to move manufacturing close to the population followed. By the early 1800s Pittsburgh, Pennsylvania, was earning a reputation as the "mid-west" glass center. Towns along the Ohio River in West Virginia, an area that remained a part of the state of Virginia until 1863, were quick to usurp some of the Pittsburgh skilled glass labor, to utilize available local natural coal resources, and grasp the significance of easy river transportation. Thus, towns like Wheeling and Wellsburg in West Virginia became competitors for some of the Pittsburgh glass business early in the nineteenth century.

It is as a part of this rich history of glass production in the Ohio River valley that the story of L. G. Wright Glass Co. is told. Innovations and available labor from the Wheeling glass houses created a legacy in pressed glass that nurtured nearby firms like New Martinsville Glass, Fenton Art Glass™, Erskine Glass, Riverside Glass, and literally dozens of others. The story of Wright Glass begins within one of these Ohio River glass houses, New Martinsville Glass Co.

New Martinsville Glass Company opened in 1900 to produce pressed glass. The substantial brick factory was near the Ohio River and immediately beside the railroad in New Martinsville, West Virginia. Lawrence Gale "Si" Wright was born near New Martinsville in 1904. By the mid-1930s he had returned home from a brief "seeking his fortune" sojourn in the Akron, Ohio, area rubber factories.

What did a young man with no particular trade skills, and in the midst of the Great Depression, do in rural West Virginia for a living? Clues to answer this for "Si" Wright are many. The Wright archive papers include invoices for sales from the Paden City Pottery. One dated 11 March 1935 is to the McCrory dime store in Clarksburg, West Virginia. The typed invoice has a footnote that "Wright" was the salesman and his earned commission on the small $21.70 sale was 51 cents. This is earlier than other reports have placed Wright back home and he was clearly already on the road as a traveling salesman.

L. G. Wright's business card when he worked as a representative for New Martinsville Glass. Circa mid-1930s.

It is reported that he assumed the job as one of the traveling salesmen for the New Martinsville Glass Co. in 1936. The earliest New Martinsville Glass Mfg. Co. invoices in the WVMAG archives, which indeed cite Wright as the salesman, are dated March 11, 1936. Note that at no time was Wright limited to selling just one type of product or working for just one company. His abilities as salesman appear to have included china from Cumbow China Decorating of Abingdon, Virginia; Paden City Pottery of Paden City, West Virginia; New Martinsville Glass; Westmoreland Glass, Grapeville, Pennsylvania; and others. His role was similar to that of a company "rep" today, representing several and diverse lines.

Mr. Wright's commission earned from New Martinsville Glass for one month, December 1936. Note the predominance of A. A. Sales as an account.

Wright seems to spread his wings as a salesman and really begin to make contact and contracts in the 1936-1938 period. A commission statement from New Martinsville Glass dated December 1936 shows Wright had sold almost fifty orders for the New Martinsville Glass Co. that month totaling $1,501.14 and earning the young Wright $150 for his monthly commission. Not a bad salary for the time at all! Noteworthy from the December 1936 commission is that well over one third of the sales were to A. A. Sales Co, Inc. of University City, Missouri. This firm would be one of Wright's best customers for many, many years, a firm that still survives today as A. A. Importing™.

```
                    WHOLESALE TO DEALERS
        ANTIQUES  -  PATTERN GLASS  -  NOVELTIES  -  STAMPS

                    A.A.SALES CO.inc
                      6508 DELMAR BLVD.
                     UNIVERSITY CITY, MO.
        JULY 4TH    193 7                    PHONE CAbany 0270

Mr Lawrence Right
New martinsville West Va.

Dear Si.-

You know doubt wonder why I have not written to you regard-
ing my coming to New Martinsville. I have waited purposely
a few days to see what is wrong with my 2 smaller children.
They both have contracted a bad case of whooping cough which
you know lasts several weeks. Due to this and to my being so
heavily stocked with goodsI thought it best to postpone my
trip until some time in August probably the the latter part.
Write me when you get back and will be at leisure the latter part of
August. Dont misunderstand me about being heavily stocked.It is
not the goods that worries me but the place to put the goods.
You saw how heavy I am stocked and short of space in addition
I received 5 barrels of Turkies also 21 barrels due from
New Martinsville Tuesday and over 30 cases and barrels of
other goods arrived since you left St.Louis Mo. So any thing
you can do for me during the next Few weeks I will greatly
appreciate it.

I was greatly dissapointed in your factory holding up my ship-
ment of hats and goblets for so long. I RECEIVED A SPECIAL DELIVERY
LETTER FROM ONE OF MY CUSTOMERS IN CONN. TELLING ME THAT MY
BIG HATS WERE OUT AND OFFERED FOR SALE ONE WEEK BEFORE YOUR
FACTORY SHIPPED ME GOOS. You got the jump on me there no
doubt. However I think it fair and reasonable to ask you
not to sell my hats to Jobbers, Paul Thomas , Furguson or
any of my customers that you know are my customers. In re-
turn I will do the same for you on your Moon and star goblets
and any other items that you care to let me have.   Please let
me know if you have allready sold these people. I hope you will
let me know at once.

When will we get some moon and star goblets. By all means get
that big slipper out.I get calls for them daily.When will your
factory ship me the Amber large hats.So far they have only
shipped Vasaline and Blue and they are due to arrive Tuesday.
I can now use One barrel of Westward Ho Goblets.Please ship
with the Copper lustre that you said you will send me.Ship
by freight. CAREFULLY EXAMINE YOUR WESTWARD HO SAUCE DISHES.
I HAVE FOUND MANY WITH SMALL CRACKS AND LARGE CRACKS.THE SMALL
CRACKS GET LARGER WHEN RATTLED OR BUMPED. I wrote for a better
price on these or privilege to return the bad ones.
```

Original correspondence between A. A. Sales and Wright in 1937. Note that A. A. Gralnick, the "A.A." of A. A. Sales, has yet learned to tell Wright from Right! Note the mention of Ruth Webb Lee, who was at this time writing extensively about "reproductions" of pressed glass and the tip to Wright to "say less to Fenton" about the "reproductions." This is a telling letter by any interpretation.

```
                    WHOLESALE TO DEALERS
        ANTIQUES  -  PATTERN GLASS  -  NOVELTIES  -  STAMPS

                    A.A.SALES CO.inc
                      6508 DELMAR BLVD.
                     UNIVERSITY CITY, MO.
                    193_                    PHONE CAbany 0270

Please get this.The less you say to Fenton about reproductions
the better off we will both be.If we leave them alone and
dont make them to wise, they will make their reproductions
better than the old ones and they make the wrong colors
which will help our sales on the items you make for me in the
right colors.

You know the right colors will sell these items. Let them
make cape Cod green and wisteria and Gold.They are not good colors
though some can be sold.

I am still dickering with enos Glass co regarding there Rose
and snow mold.The lowest price I can get it for is $75.00
in addition I have to buy all of their blue Goblets about
25 Dz at a profit. I expect to own this mould this week and
will write you when I have same and will ship to you to make
colors.

Received the Turkies. DO NOT LIKE THE ROSE COLOR AND THEY INSIST
I HAVE TO TAKE ALL THE ROSE THEY HAVE ON HAND TO GET PROTECTION.
IT WILL NOT SELL. I am not worried about the dozen sent me
but I do not want any more of that color. Your name is on the
invoice as salesman and you should get the commission.It will
not make you rich but I hope you will write them to send you
same.

Those two Ruth Webb Lee items we discussed, Negro on the
Railroad tracks and the other one please find out if this
party will make me a bout a dozen of each in clear for samples.
Will pay for these and then negotaite for quantity in colors.
If we work together inHARMONY we will both be better off
as between us two we can talk Turn lots and quatities and any
factory will have respect for you and give you better prices
when you talk that way.

ONE THING I WOULD LIKE TO GET FROM FENTON AND YOU CAN TAKE
PART OF THEM AND THAT IS CRANBERRY FROSTED DOT TUMBLERS. I CAN
NO DO ANY GOOD THRU MAIL.THEY QUOTE ME 3.75 DZ WHICH IS TO
HIGH. NEGOTAITE WITH THEM FOR A TURN OF THEM AND THE PRICE WE
CAN GET BY WITH IS 3.00 DZ LESS 10%. I think on direct con-
versation you can put this over. TELL THEM YOU WANT THE DEEP
CRANBERRY RED NOT LIGHT. I would not buy any Pitchers or
Bowls as they are to heavy and clumsy to ship and handle. You
can do better with samller items items.
```

```
                    WHOLESALE TO DEALERS
        ANTIQUES  -  PATTERN GLASS  -  NOVELTIES  -  STAMPS

                    A.A.SALES CO.inc
                      6508 DELMAR BLVD.
                     UNIVERSITY CITY, MO.
                    193_ 3                   PHONE CAbany 0270

We ca both make money if we work in Harmony and do not spep
on each others toes. It is better for you and I both to lose
a sale than hurt each others feelings. Naturally I hated to see
my hats sold 10 days before I could even get one, and it being my
mold. I certainly will mention again that I did not like the
slippers in a dept store in K.C. or any being sold to Dennis
Moore and so forth.I bought enough of them to get protection
on this mold together with the mold thrown in in addition
to the many other goods bought from your factory. Also your
factory should not ship orders of slippers to small ealers-
dealers of a few at a time.These shold have been sent to me or
you if you want them. I have 2 customers write me if I did
not give them better service they would get them direct from
New Martinsville.

I have not written Harry regarding any of the above. I would
want you to get these items straightened out and let me know accord-
ingly.

Some factory makes a milk glass covered fish.Have you ever
knwon who they are.

Let me know when you get married. You are bound to do so now.
I dont think you can back out.

Excuse this writing as I am writing on July 4 th and the girl is
gone. By all means let us get the barber bottle mold. I will
make you an easy proposition. I will furnish Rose and snow
mold Goblet and you get the Barber bottle Hob nail mold
and finish it up. I think that is better than making the Rose
and snow mold.IF YOU AGREE TO THIS LET ME KNOW. DO NOT SELL ONE
BOTTLE UNTIL I SEE THE SAMPLE. MY REASON WE MIGHT WORK THIS OUT
BETWEEN US TO SELL ONLY ONE AT A TIME AND GET A GOOD PRICE FOR IT
AND IF IT IS GOOD WE WILL SELL NO MORE THAN I PAIR TO A DEALER.
This mold fixed up will cost you much less than I pay for the
Goblet mold.Advise if accepted.

I do not intens to sell my large hats in quantities.I will sell
only One to 3 to a customer at a time. If they order more than one o
color I will tell them I have only one of aolor left and to reorer
in 10 Days.That makes them scarce and more desireable. When a custom
er can get all they want of a item then they dont want it so bad.

Please answer this long letter soon as you can in detail
With best wishes,
I am Yours truly,
A.A. GRALNICK
```

A. A. Sales invoices from New Martinsville Glass noting "Wright" as salesman. Noteworthy are the items being manufactured and the prices.

7

It has been written that 1938 was the beginning of Wright glass, but correspondence and records relating to the L. G. Wright Co. exist by at least June of 1937. In any event it was for unknown reasons that L.G. "Si" Wright struck out on his own. He had for some time prior combined salesmanship for New Martinsville Glass with peddling diverse other wares. Perhaps his independent success encouraged him. But it seems likely that the sale of New Martinsville Glass Company in July 1938 led to some separation between Wright and the new management.

All the time Wright had worked for New Martinsville, the company had been in court managed receivership and under the control of local men, men Wright likely knew well. In 1938 a sale under bankruptcy places New Martinsville Glass in the hands of Carl Schultz and R.M. Rice of Connecticut. These men were affiliated with the successful Silver City Glass Company, a New England based glass decorator. Operations resumed at New Martinsville Glass in August 1938 under the new management (*China, Glass and Lamps,* 1938) but one can safely presume it was without L. G. Wright.

What was Wright selling in that early period? Without real catalogs per se we can piece together some facts from the archival papers we have, and these are telling.

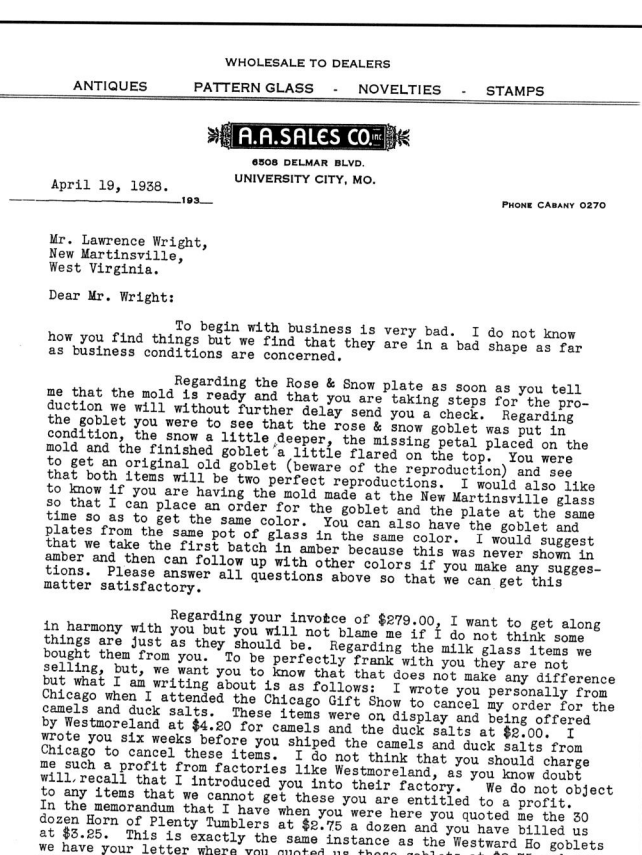

Correspondence from A. A. Sales to Wright in 1938. Note the suggestion of getting an old Rose & Snow goblet to insure the reproduction is close to the original.

Reply to an inquiring correspondence in 1938 notes several pressed glass items and prices.

Flier illustrating the Westward-Ho goblet. Paul Thomas is one of the clients of A. A. Sales that A. A. asked Wright to not approach. The source of the goblet from A. A. and Wright seems interconnected at least.

A. A. SALES CO. Inc. letter (page 2):

Mr. Lawrence Wright,

- 2 -

Now Mr. Wright I am not writing you these complaints because business is dull and we are not selling the merchandise but I hope you will fully understand my sincercity in getting our transactions straightened out so that their will be good feelings on both sides. I will greatly appreciate if you will send me a credit on the camels and duck salts and that you will see my side of it. I am not wirting this to letter to fish for time as I know your bill is due. To show our good faith I am sending you a check for $200.00 on account, but, bear in mind that I want to work in harmony with you and if these things were reversed I certainly would look at it in the same light.

You noodoubt know from our dealings that I am not very good on answering letters but if you would write more often I would improve.

Regarding the New England Pineapple goblet kindly advise if I can display this item on my circular. I have done exactly as I have promised you and have not displayed this item nor the Baltimore Pear. The Pineapple goblet is not a very good seller in as much as Ruth Webb Lee is showing a large picture of this goblet as a reproduction which hurts the sale of this item. I realize that I could go ahead and put it on my circular but I promised you that I would not do it and will be governed with what reply you make. We have sold the Baltimore Pear Goblets and could use a few more as we have quite a few dealers coming into the store that would buy them.

I also want it clearly understood between us that I am always to own the rose & snow goblet which I own and that you are always to own the rose & snow plate. Also understand that on the plate mold I am to pay $75.00 as my part of the plate mold, but please acknowledge in your next writing that we are both to have the use of both the goblet and plate mold at any time you or I may desire to have any glass made up from it. You were to pay the cost of having the goblet mold changed and the balance of the plate mold. These facts I would like to have clearly understood so that there will be no futuner-misunderstandings.

Sit down and write me a nice long letter answering all my questions.

With kindest regards, I am,

Yours very truly,

A. A. SALES CO. Inc.

An April 1937 letter from Stone Hardware in Cincinnati, Ohio, notes a Westward Ho compote and a Three Face lamp in the correspondence.

A June 1937 invoice from Morgantown Glass Works to L. G. Wright shows they had pressed twenty dozen Westward Ho footed sauce dishes at a cost of $3.00 per dozen.

A June 1937 order to L. G. Wright from the Virgin and Virgin Mercantile Co. of Omaha, Nebraska, included:
  Turkeys, covered dish in crystal and colors
  Daisy and Button goblets in Vaseline
  Hat, pint and quart sizes in crystal

THE L. G. WRIGHT COMPANY

MANUFACTURERS OF

PRESSED AND BLOWN GLASSWARE

NEW MARTINSVILLE, W. VA.

SOLD BY

CUSTOMER ORDER DATE
CUSTOMER ORDER NO.
DATE SHIPPED

SOLD TO W. Lester Boward
         6 Harrison St.
         Cumberland, Md.

SHIPPED TO

ROUTE SHIPPED Express

TERMS: 1% 15 days, 30 days Net.

SHIPPING DATE June 1, 1938

ALL GOODS SOLD F. O. B. NEW MARTINSVILLE, W. VA. NO ALLOWANCE FOR BREAKAGE. CLAIMS FOR OVERCHARGES MUST BE MADE IMMEDIATELY ON RECEIPT OF GOODS.

PACKAGES	DOZ.	DESCRIPTION	PRICE	AMOUNT	TOTAL
	6 only	Moon and Star Goblets	.75	4.50	
	6 only	Fruit Goblets	.75	4.50	
	2 only	Rose and Snow Plates Crystal	1.25	2.50	
		Total		11.50	
				$11.39	

Wright invoice in 1938 for pressed glass. Amazing is the small quantities ordered by various dealers. Here items in quantities of six and two were shipped.

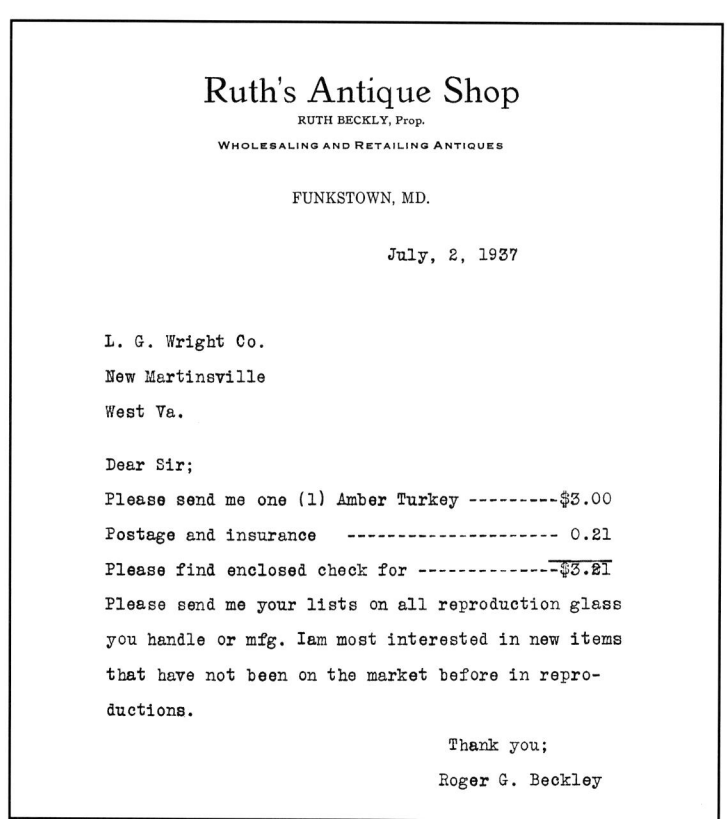

Shipment to one of the hundreds of antique shops found in the Wright papers. This 1937 invoice is for "one (1) Amber Turkey"!

The first Wright photos of products date from 1947 when Pappas Brothers of Parkersburg, West Virginia, traveled to the Wright site in New Martinsville to capture the images. In these early photos crystal was photographed in black and white and colored glass in color. The photographic images were used to ease the sales pitches of Wright's traveling sales staff. They struggled to set up and pack, time after time, physical samples of the glass and the use of large, color photographs was much simpler and easier.

NO. 70 COVERED CANDY BOXES

70-5 FLAT IRON CANDY BOX
Amber, Blue, Green, Amethyst

70-11 STOVE CANDY BOX
Amber, Blue, Green, Amethyst

70-12 TURTLE LARGE
Amber, Green
Milk Glass

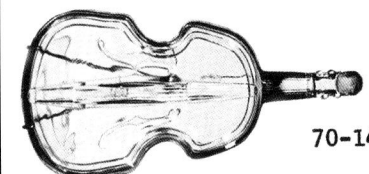

70-14 VIOLIN CANDY BOX
Amber, Blue, Green, Amethyst

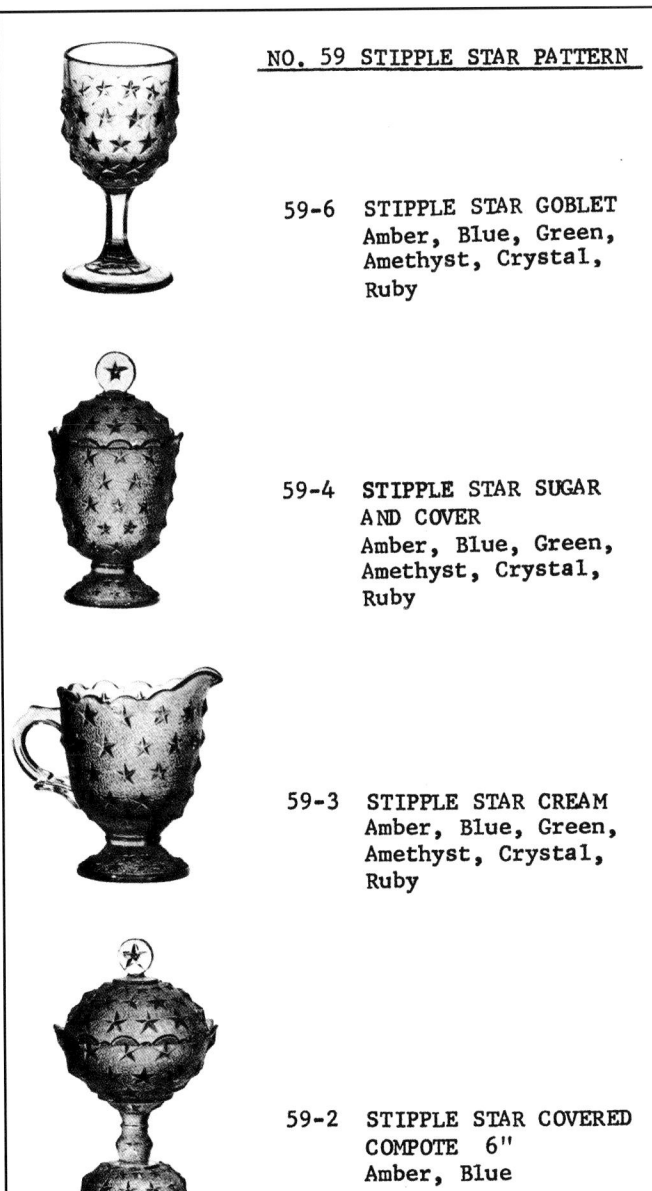

NO. 59 STIPPLE STAR PATTERN

59-6 STIPPLE STAR GOBLET
Amber, Blue, Green, Amethyst, Crystal, Ruby

59-4 STIPPLE STAR SUGAR AND COVER
Amber, Blue, Green, Amethyst, Crystal, Ruby

59-3 STIPPLE STAR CREAM
Amber, Blue, Green, Amethyst, Crystal, Ruby

59-2 STIPPLE STAR COVERED COMPOTE 6"
Amber, Blue

These loose leaf, black and white pages are among the various attempts at making a catalog Wright explored over time.

The early 1960s saw a return of the Pappas photographers and new color images for Wright. For each photo a mimeographed page of captions and prices was created to accompany the images in the large black binders. These photos in the large binders would serve for many years as the salesman's catalogs; new captions and pricing listings were made to reflect changes over time, but the same photos were retained. This pre-dated published catalogs, the first being printed in 1968. It was also in 1968 that Wright opened its own decorating department.

L.G. "Si" Wright passed away 22 August 1969 in his sixty-fifth year. While the company had been born of his vision and sustained by his energy, his wife proved capable of meeting any challenge. She continued the business for the next twenty years.

Mrs. Verna Mae Wright saw the introduction of carnival glass in the early 1970s, the creation in 1971 of a wonderful Wright logo plate in a bread plate form, and in 1974 heeded the call of collectors to mark at least some of the Wright production with the letter "W" in a circle. Her stewardship of L. G. Wright lasted until her death in 1990.

Upon the death of Mrs. Wright, the company passed to the Wright's heirs, they having had no children. Verna Mae Wright's cousin Dorothy Stephan and Phyllis Stephan Beuttner, the daughter of Dorothy, led this phase of the company. These two ladies, not experienced in the glass business, continued the business through nearly a decade of tough times for American glass. It is noteworthy that a number of loyal employees remained at Wright, some spanning all three periods of ownership. Certainly some measure of the success of Wright glass is due to the loyalty, product knowledge, diligent work, and good counsel given by the New Martinsville residents who worked at Wright Glass. The company was still selling items a short time before the final auction in 1999.

Wright flier made to mail to potential customers. No date, but this circa 1960-70s imprint uses diversity of products and color to make this a powerful sales tool.

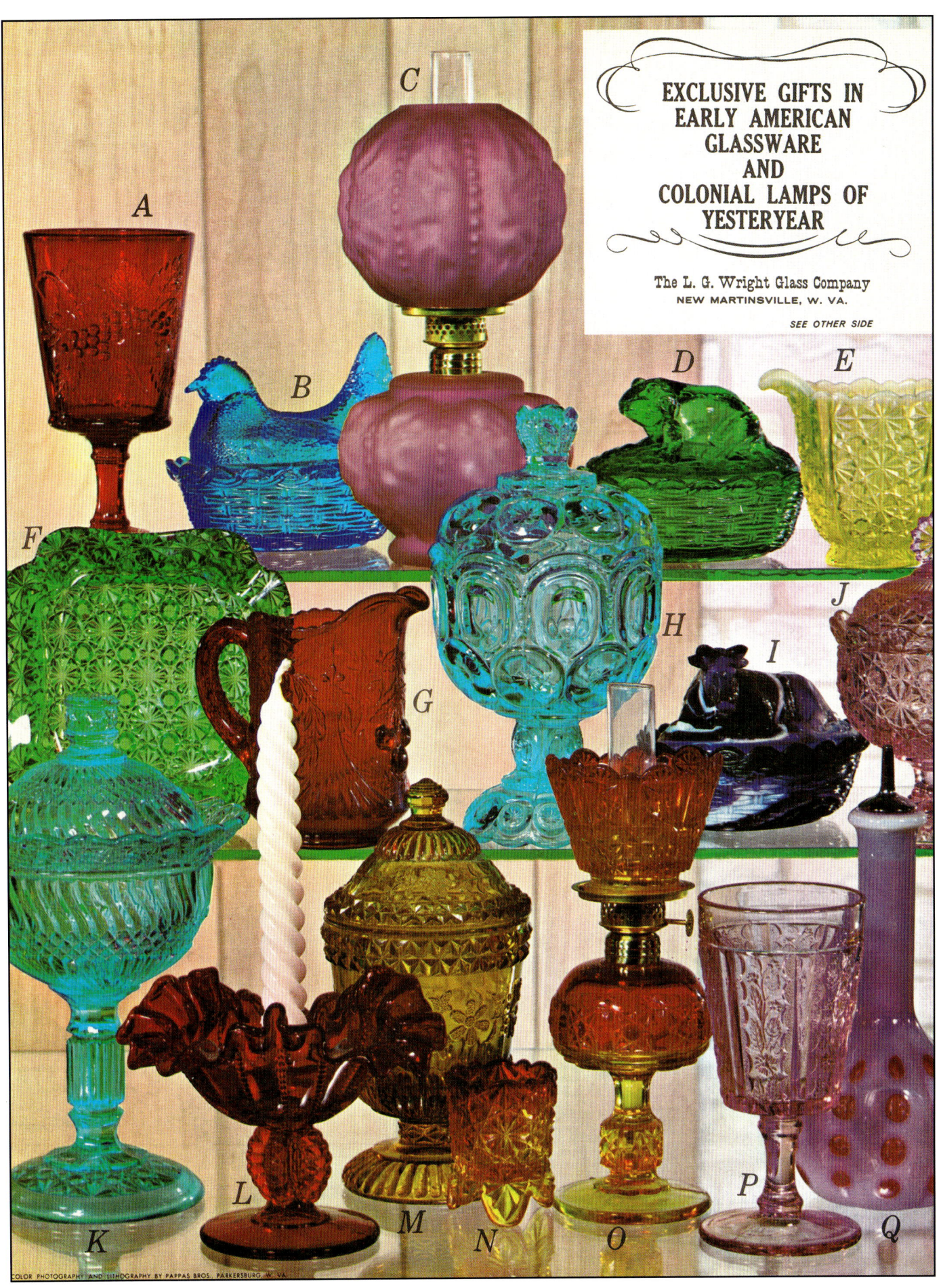

One of the Wright mail inserts, again undated but circa 1960-70s.

Wright product development was often best found on the cover to their catalog supplements. This 1975 cover includes predominately lamps, a major part of the line throughout time, although not dealt with in this book.

Wright offered a great variety of "Tiffany" styled lamps as shown by this cover to their 1976 catalog supplement.

The 1978 catalog supplement cover mixes the leaded "Tiffany" styled lamps and a popular hen on nest in opalescent.

Wright 1979 catalog supplement cover returns to the balance of hand painted lamps and giftware.

17

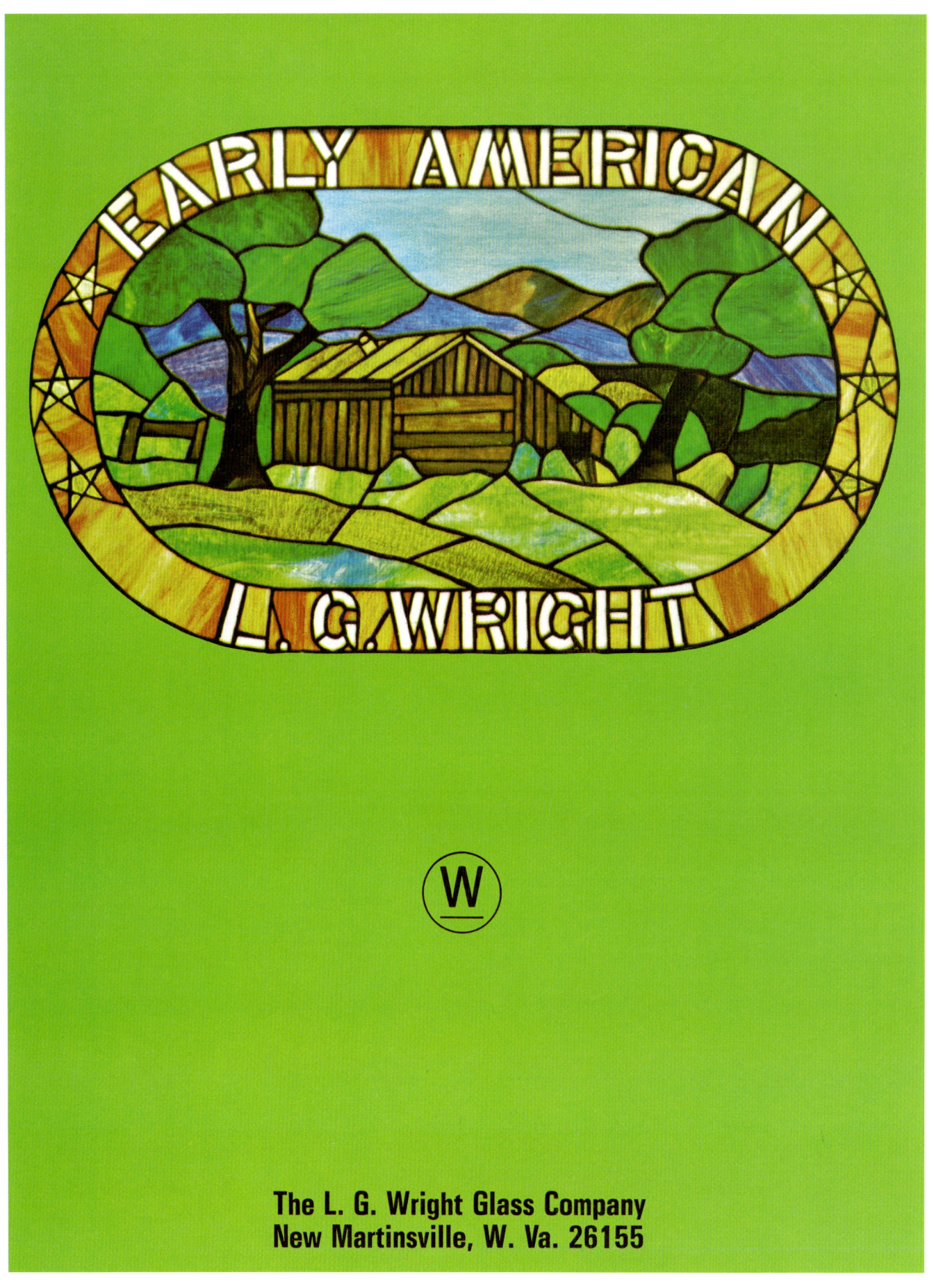

**The L. G. Wright Glass Company
New Martinsville, W. Va. 26155**

This leaded panel was displayed in the factory and shows the small barn which Wright used as a warehouse in the earliest years. This is the same image found on the Wright dealer bread plate. Also featured is the "W" trademark adopted with reportedly strong urgings from Fenton.

THE L. G. WRIGHT GLASS CO.

"Cherished Today—Treasured Tomorrow"

The Wright facility in New Martinsville, West Virginia. Off to the right is the Wright home.

One image of the products being assembled at the Wright factory the very day of the final auction.

From the final auction in 1999 is this image of lamp parts. All was auctioned.

Auction photo, 1999. Note the amber cased and satinized vase, the opalescent lamps, and the cranberry opalescent covered apothecaries.

Wright final auction photo of one of the many tables of ware.

Inside the Wright showroom the day of the 1999 auction.

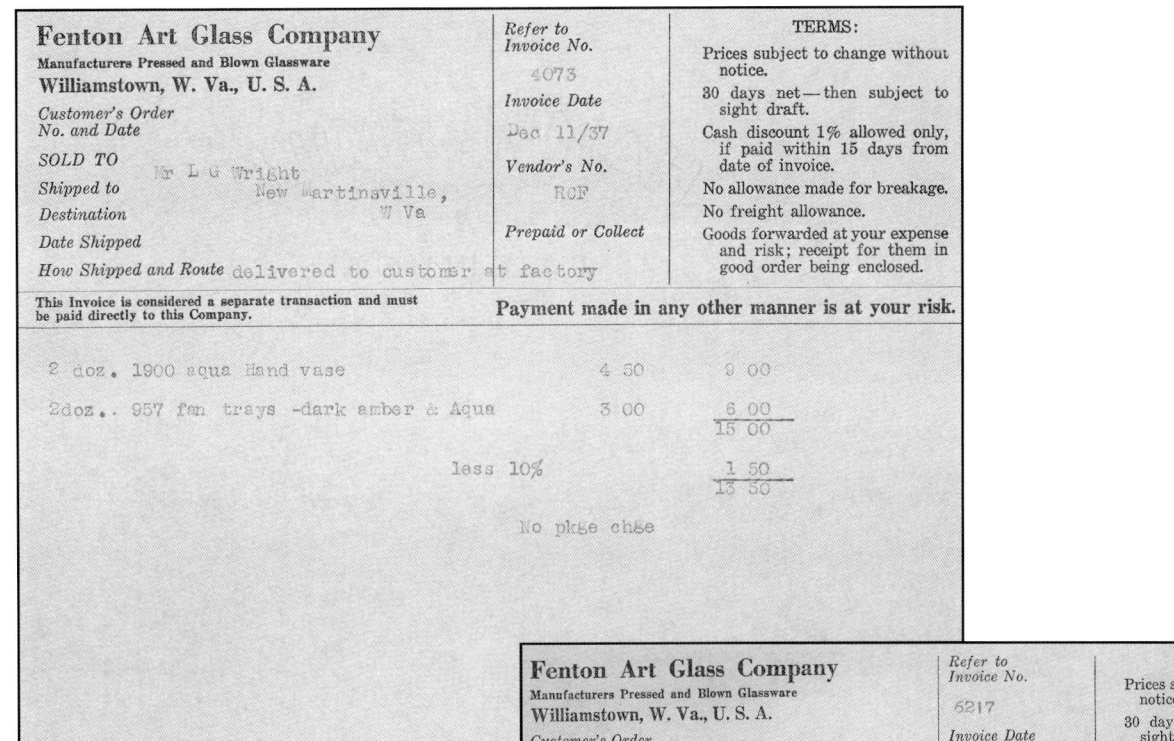

Original Fenton Invoices from the 1930s showing what was being made, the small quantities, and the prices.

23

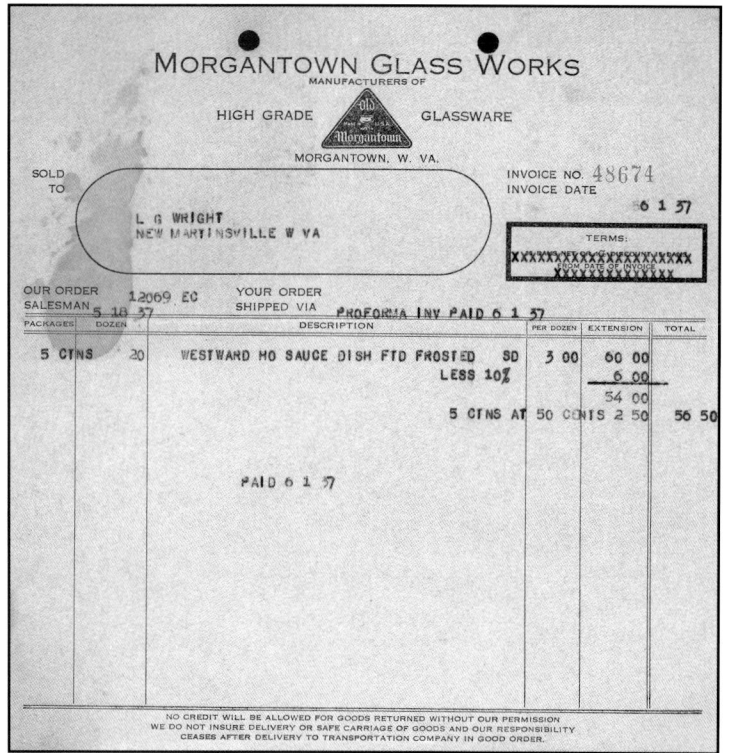

Original Invoice from Morgantown Glass Works for pressing Westward Ho sauce dishes in 1937. Note the cost of $3.00 per dozen or roughly a quarter a piece.

Fenton Art Glass, Williamstown, West Virginia: Opalescent, cranberry, more and endless pressed items, 1930s until the end; Custard and carnival, 1970s.
Fostoria Glass, Moundsville, West Virginia: Miscellaneous ware in the 1930s, pink Moon & Star and Daisy & Button patterns.
Gibson Glass, Milton, West Virginia: Free form art line included in the catalogs of the 1980s.
Indiana Glass, Dunkirk, Indiana: WVMAG has receipts for Kings Crown wines, goblets, and Lords Supper bread plates in the 1930s.
Morgantown Glass, Morgantown, West Virginia: known to have pressed Westward Ho sauces and other pieces.
Mosser Glass, Cambridge, Ohio.
New Martinsville Glass, New Martinsville, West Virginia.
Paden City Glass, Paden City, West Virginia: $1,100 worth of business in 1941.
Rodefer Glass Co., Bellaire, Ohio.
Summit Glass Co., Ohio.
Viking Glass, New Martinsville, West Virginia.
Venetian Glass Corporation, Rochester, Pennsylvania: cased and blown circa 1953 on.
Westmoreland Glass, Grapeville, Pennsylvania: Kitten plates & rabbit plates as per 1930s inventory; chocolate and carnival glass during the 1970s.
Wilkerson Glass Co., Moundsville, West Virginia.

Who Made the Glass L. G. Wright Sold?

The question of who made glass for Wright is a complex one indeed. Over the decades almost anyone capable of making handmade glass was a potential producer for Wright. The archives at WVMAG have some wonderful late in time information: here an index card represents each shape/mould owned and the notes indicate who made the piece, when, and in what colors and quality. It is like reading a mystery novel as the next card, at times even the same card, introduces new players and an almost endless cast of characters. The following list includes those known and documented producers of hot glass for L. G. Wright:

Bailey Glass Co., Morgantown, West Virginia.
Beaumont Glass, Morgantown, West Virginia.
Cambridge Glass, Cambridge, Ohio: specifically covered turkeys in the 1930s.
Central Glass Co., Wheeling, West Virginia: tumblers per correspondence in WVMAG archives.
Davis-Lynch Glass, Morgantown, West Virginia: Lamp parts, larger covered opal/milk glass objects, and hand decorated wares.
Dalzell-Viking, New Martinsville, West Virginia.
Erskine Glass, Wellsburg, West Virginia: covered animal dishes in the 1930s.

Westmoreland		Thistle Water Pitcher	W1611
6/7/78	162		
11/13/78	216		
8/14/79	216		
8-14-80	196		
5/27/82	34		

Plum Glass		God & Home Water Pitcher	
Date	Blue Slag		
10/1/90	82		
10/8/90	14 seconds		

W905 Grape & Cable 6" Oval Bowl   Boyd Glass

Date	Ameth Carnival
2-21-94	470
2-17-94	640

W31 Moon & Star Sugar Shaker   Pennsboro Glass

Date	Crystal
7-27-90	72
12-5-90	273
4-28-93	216

Tee Pee Cruet   Gibson Glass

Date	Red Slag	Date	Blue Slag	Date	Green Sl	Date	Ameth Sl
5-9-91	19	10-4-91	17	10-4-91	10	5-16-91	3
5-16-91	1	10-19-93	4	10-3-91	10	5-20-91	14
5-20-91	2	10-29-93	5			10-13-93	3
10-19-93	7					10-14-93	10
10-29-93	2					7-19-93	12
2-2-95	9						
3-29-95	4						

FENTON   Eye Winker Marmalade Jar   W1316

1982	Crystal
10/8	250

W97 Moon & Star Salt & Pepper   Pennsboro Glass Co.

Date	Crystal
7-27-90	240

Fenton   Fluted Barber Bottle   W1431

1978	Vas. Fern	1978	Blue Fern	1978	Cran Fern
10-30	244	12-20	261		
1980		1980			
10/16	61	10/24	56		
	335	1981			
		4/21	165		

Examples of the production cards acquired by WVMAG from the Wright auction showing the piece made, the date it was produced and the quantity as well as the glass company that made it at that specific moment in time for Wright.

Westmoreland		Cherry Tumbler			W 255
1982	Caramel Slag	1982	Slag	1982	Deco.
2-4	31				
4-28					

Mosser Glass		Three Face Sugar Shaker	W384
19788 6/20	Crystal 303		
1979			
2-8	294		
9/11	303		
8-8-80	303		
7-31-81	324		
10/27/82	341		
2/12/85	167		
3/31/88	216		
9-22-89	225		

WESTMORELAND	Blue Opal	Cherry Tumbler			Black Opalescent	W255
3/23/78	15	1978 3/27	Deco 190	1979 8/8	Slag 226	
5/4/78	161			1981 5/14	129	
5/4/78	135					
5/24/78	296					
8/15/78	100					
		1979 6/14	Deco 500			
		1981 8-2	164			
		9-11	13			

MOSSER	THREE FACE TOOTHPICK	W379
1979 9/11	580	
1980		
3-21	545	
11/21	699	
1982 10/27	574	
1985 2/12	553	
1988 9-9	868	

VIKING		MOON & STAR SPOONER		44-37	W96	
1978	Ruby	Amber	Blue	Cry	Va.	Pink
1/12	117			1978 3/22	323	
10/13	224					
1980						
1/30	218					
1981						
11/7	342					
1983						
7/28	311					

Moon & Star 5oz. Juice Glass — Wilkerson Glass

Date	Crystal
4/29/93	50

W34 Daisy & button Canoe — Wilkerson Glass

Date	Crystal
12-10-90	54
9-2-92	61
	3 seconds

Davis & Lynch 6814 7" Moon & Star

11/10/88	12
9/3/91	12

W712 Peacock Bowl — Summit Art Glass

Date	Amethyst Carnival
2-12-94	363
2-18-94	385
2-19-94	242
2-22-94	132
4-8-94	118

Quality Glass — W13 Pear Fount - Opal — Cost 5.00

2/27/85	127
8/85	60
7/18/85	72
3/25/86	43

L. G. WRIGHT and "Early American" Pattern Glass Goblets

The correspondence now in the archives at WVMAG between Wright and several prominent antique dealers across the country leaves little to the imagination as they strive to make the Wright goblets accurate copies of their original nineteenth century counterparts. What follows is an attempt to generate a list of the known Pressed Glass Goblets made by Wright. It is surely not complete but is a necessary lesson for all students of Pattern Glass. Remember that a piece made in 1890 and a piece made in 1940 may today bear strikingly similar signs of wear and age, making the distinctions sometimes far from easy. The known patterns include:

Acorn Goblet
#77-17: known made in amber, crystal, blue. Found in archive, original photo c. 1960s.

Artichoke Goblet
#77-18: known made in crystal with satin. Found in archive, original photo c. 1960s.

Baltimore Pear Goblet
#77-112: appears in the 1938 inventory.

Broken Column Goblet
#77-102: known made in crystal, archive original photo c. 1960s.

Cabbage Leaf Goblet
#77-19: known made in crystal satin. Illustrated in the 1968 purple catalog.

Cabbage Rose Goblet
no number found: known made in crystal. Archive original photo c. 1960s.

Cardinal Goblet
#76-1: known made in crystal and ruby. Illustrated in 1975 supplement.

Cherry Goblet
#7-12: known made in crystal. Illustrated in 1976 supplement, slag in 1977 supplement, and in amber, blue, green, and ruby in the purple catalog.

Daisy & Button Thumbprint Panel Goblet
#22-30: known made in ruby stained, illustrated in the 1976 supplement, crystal amber, blue, green, pink, amethyst, amberina, ruby, Vaseline opalescent in the purple catalog.

Daisy & Button Goblet with plain stem
#22-29: known made in amber and blue and appearing from the 1938 inventory to the purple catalog.

Daisy & Cube Goblet
#77-21: known made in amber ,blue, crystal, green, amberina, and ruby as illustrated in the purple catalog.

Daisy & Cube, Etched
#77-22: known made in amber, blue, crystal and green in the purple catalog.

Dahlia Goblet
#2-3: known made in crystal as illustrated in the 1978 supplement.

Deer & Pine Tree Goblet
#77-103: known made in crystal. Archive original photo c. 1960s.

Diamond Quilted Goblet
#77-23: known made in amber, blue, green, amberina, and ruby as illustrated in the purple catalog and in amethyst, dark green, amber, and ruby in archive original photo c. 1960s.

Double Wedding Ring Goblet
#11-2: known made in crystal as illustrated in the 1977 supplement.

Eyewinker Goblet
#25-3: known made in crystal and amber, blue, crystal, green, and ruby in the purple catalog.

Frosted Ribbon Goblet
#77-104: known made in crystal satin, original photo c. 1960s.

Grasshopper Goblet
#77-24: known made in amber, in the purple catalog and amber, crystal, blue, and green as illustrated in original photo, c. 1960s.

Herringbone Goblet
#77-25: known made in ruby, amber, and green, as illustrated in a 1967 photo.

Hobnail Goblet
#33-8: known made in amber, blue, green, amethyst, and ruby, as per the purple catalog.

Horn of Plenty Goblet
#77-26: known made in crystal as illustrated in original 1960s photo and ruby in 1967 photo.

Inverted Dot Goblet
#77-27: known made in amber, blue, and dark green in a 1967 original photo where it was captioned "discontinued by 1967."

Jersey Swirl Goblet
#35-5: known made in crystal as illustrated in the purple catalog, also in amber, blue, crystal, green, and ruby.

King's Crown Goblet
no number found: made in crystal and ruby stain as shown in original photo, c. 1960s.

Lion Goblet
#77-28: known made in crystal satin, shown in 1938 inventory and purple catalog.

Maple Leaf Goblet
#77-29: known made in crystal, blue, dark green, and amber as illustrated in original photo, c. 1960s.
Mirror & Rose Goblet
#77-79: known made in amber, green, pink, and ruby, as illustrated in purple catalog.
Moon & Star Goblet
#44-22: known made in crystal as listed in 1938 inventory, amber in 1967 color photo where it was captioned "discontinued," and amber, blue, crystal, green, pink, amethyst, ruby, and Vaseline opalescent in purple catalog.
New England Pineapple Goblet
no number found: known made in crystal and listed on 1938 inventory and in original photo, 1960s.
One-O-One Goblet
#77-42: known made in crystal as per original 1960s photo.
Panel Daisy Goblet
#77-31: known made in amber, blue, crystal, pink, and ruby as per purple catalog and crystal in original photo, 1960s.
Priscilla Goblet
#55-62: known made in crystal as illustrated in purple catalog and amber, blue, green, crystal, and ruby in the purple catalog.
Panel Thistle Goblet
no number found: known made in amber, crystal, dark green, and blue. Archive original photo c. 1960s
Panel Grape Goblet (Note: *Not* called Paneled Grape by Wright)
#55-7: known made in crystal, amber, blue, green and amberina, ruby, and Vaseline opalescent as illustrated in the purple catalog and milk glass, crystal, dark green, blue, ruby, and amber in original photo, circa 1960s, and originally as early as the 1938 inventory.
Plume
no number found: Crystal, crystal(satin), original photo c. 1960s.
Princess Feather
#77-33: amber, blue, and crystal, original photo c. 1960s. Captioned discontinued in 1967.
Ribbed Palm Leaf
#77-98: amber, green, and ruby, purple catalog.
Rose and Snow
no number found: 1938 inventory, assorted colors.
Rose Sprig
no number found: Blue, crystal, amber, original photo c. 1960s

"S" Goblet
#77-34: amber, green, amethyst, and ruby, purple catalog.
Sawtooth Goblet
#77-35: crystal, amber, blue, crystal, green, pink, amberina, dark blue, and ruby, purple catalog.
Shell & Tassel Goblet
no number found: Crystal, original photo c. 1960s.
Stork Goblet
#77-114: crystal only, 1974 supplement.
Strawberry & Currant Goblet
#77-36: green, ruby, blue, amethyst, amber, Vaseline opalescent, purple catalog.
Stippled Star
#59-6: amber, blue, crystal, green, amberina, and ruby in the purple catalog; blue, crystal, green, amber, and amethyst in a c. 1960s photo.
Sweetheart
#77-37: amber, blue, crystal, and ruby, purple catalog.
Thistle "L.G. Goblet"
#64-38: crystal, 1978 supplement, purple catalog.
Three Face Goblet
#65-3: crystal (satin), 1938 inventory, purple catalog.
Thousand Eye Goblet
no number found: blue, amber, crystal, original photo circa 1960s.
Thumbprint Goblet
no number found: 1938 inventory.
Tree of Life Goblet with eternal flame stem
#60-4: found in amber, crystal, and blue, purple catalog.
Two Panel Goblet
#77-39: known made in amber and crystal, original photo c. 1960s.
Westward Ho Goblet
#66-3: crystal (satin), 1938 inventory, purple catalog.
Wildflower Goblet
#67-5: Vaseline opalescent, purple catalog; amber, crystal, and blue, original photo c. 1960s.
Wildrose Goblet
#77-41: Vaseline, 1976 supplement; crystal, 1977 supplement; ruby, amber, pink, green, amethyst, and blue, purple catalog; amber, blue, green, amethyst, pink, and ruby, photo 1967.
Wheat & Barley Goblet
#77-40: amber and blue, original photo, salesman 1967, captioned discontinued in 1967.

L. G. Wright Glass Co. Mold Disposition

The L. G. Wright Glass Co. was well known for making reproduction patterns. They also developed a few original patterns. The company began by selling reproductions, especially in concert with A. A. Sales (later A. A. Importing) in 1938. Correspondence between the two companies indicated they were cooperating with the ordering and selling of reproductions, sometimes even to the extent of discussing whether the reproduction was accurate or whether the color was true to the old color.

L. G. Wright Glass Co. purchased, and then resold, items from companies such as items from Fenton, the covered animal dishes from Westmoreland, and some Moon & Star pattern pieces. L. G. Wright actually owned a great number of the Moon & Star pattern molds, made for them by the Weishar Mould Co. of Wheeling, West Virginia.

The company also owned several original Dugan molds, using some as they were and modifying others. In the case of the Sweetheart pattern (originally Dugan's Victor Jeweled Heart), many molds were modified or new molds for new items made to match the line. Their Thistle pattern (a copy of the Higbee pattern known as Paneled Thistle) often included a copy of the old Higbee trademark, a bee with HIG on the wings and body. The L. G. Wright mark was a less full-bodied bee with no initials on the body or wings. In some cases, such as Mirror and Rose, the pattern was original to the L. G. Wright Glass Co. and was not a copy of any earlier pattern.

Because of the confusion many of these pieces have caused over the years, it is important to know what happened to the molds when L. G. Wright Glass Co. went out of business. Molds are important assets of a glass company, and many companies are interested in buying old molds still able to be used to add pieces to their lines.

Thus, in late May of 1999, many existing glass companies had representatives at the final L. G. Wright Glass Co. dispersal sale. Bidding was spirited for several of the molds, while many others in poor condition were sold for scrap. A few were sold to people who wanted a souvenir of the company. A number of molds were still usable but were unidentified at the time of sale.

The following is a list of molds and the corresponding companies or persons who purchased them. Note that the names for patterns and pieces are as described by the company and/or auctioneer at the time of sale.

Key:
AA=AA Importing*
Alladin=Alladin Mantle Lamp Co.
Brodak=Brodak (?), Mt. Pleasant, Pennsylvania
Castle=Castle Reproductions*
Duck=Duck Soup Sales & Antiques
Fenton=Fenton Art Glass Co., Williamstown, West Virginia
Fuhrman=Fuhrman Glass Studios
Gibson=Gibson Glass Co., Milton, West Virginia
Mosser=Mosser Glass Co., Cambridge, Ohio
New Old=New Old Products
Rottreis="Red" Rottreis, Arizona (former salesman)
Rosso=Rosso Wholesale Glass, Inc.
Weishar=Weishar Enterprises, Wheeling, West Virginia
Wilkerson=Wilkerson Glass Co., Moundsville, West Virginia

*These two companies seemed to be working in concert at the Wright auction. The bidding number was reported to be that of AA Importing, but the molds were seen loaded on a Castle Reproductions truck.

Argonaut (copy of the old Nautilus, a.k.a. Argonaut Shell, pattern of Northwood)
    Butter & cover—AA or Castle
    Cream—AA or Castle
    Sugar & cover—AA or Castle
    Toothpick, stemmed jelly—Unknown
    Tumbler—AA or Castle
    5" oval bowl—AA or Castle
    10" oval bowl—AA or Castle

Baltimore Pear (copy of Adams' Gypsy pattern, a.k.a. Baltimore Pear)
    Goblet—Fenton
    Goblet—Mosser
    Plate—Wilkerson

Basketweave
    Base—Fenton
    Base & cover—Unknown
    Juice—Brodak
    One handle basket (two molds)—Mosser
    Two handle basket—Fenton
    Two handle toothpick—Gibson

Beaded, No. 3 (copy of a Northwood/Dugan pattern)
    Large bowl—Fenton
    Small bowl, two plungers-one plain, - candle—Fenton

Beaded Cherry
    Tumbler—Gibson

Beaded Grape, No. 5 (originally California, a.k.a. Beaded Grape by US Glass)
    Goblet—Fenton
    Punch Bowl—Mosser (sold as a Dugan mold)

Beaded Shell
    Mug—Gibson

Beehive
    Base & cover—Unknown

Bird
    Perfume stopper—Unknown
    Salt dip—Unknown
    Vase, tall—AA or Castle
    5" Dish cover—Unknown
    6" two handled bowl—Unknown

Butterfly
    Ash tray—AA or Castle
    Wine—AA or Castle

Cabbage Leaf (copy of old Riverside pattern)
    Compote & cover—AA or Castle
    Goblet—Unknown
    Rabbit plate—Brodak
    Wine—AA or Castle

Cannonball
    Jug—Mosser

Cardinal
    Cream—Rottreis
    Goblet—Mosser

Cherry, No. 7 (copy of Northwood's Cherry pattern)
    Bowl, low footed—AA or Castle
    Bowl, small oval—Unknown
    Butter cover—Unknown
    Compote, scroll footed—Unknown
    Cream—AA or Castle
    Goblet—AA or Castle
    Ice tea—AA or Castle
    Pitcher—AA or Castle
    Pitcher & tumbler—AA or Castle
    Salt dip—Rosso
    Sugar—Fenton
    Toothpick—Rosso
    7" Vase—Fenton
    8" Bowl—Unknown
    12" Bowl—AA or Castle

Circle Scroll
    Tumbler—Fenton

Corn Vase—Alladin Mantle

Cosmos (Dugan mold)
    Flower bowl—Fenton

Covered Animal Dishes
    Some of the covered animal dishes were purchased by members of the milk glass collectors club.
    Atterbury Duck bottom—Fenton
    Cat cover—Milk Glass Collectors
    Chick on Eggs—AA or Castle
    Dog, 5" cover—Milk Glass Collectors
    Duck, 5" base & top—Fenton
    Ferdinand base & cover—Unknown
    Fish dish & cover—Brodak
    Frog, 7" dish & cover—Milk Glass Collectors
    Hen, 5" base & cover—Mosser
    Hen, 5" cover—Milk Glass Collectors
    Hen, 7" & cover—Mosser
    Lamb, 5" dish cover—Fenton
    Owl, 5" base—Unknown
    Owl, 5" cover—Unknown
    Rabbit, 5" dish & base—Milk Glass Collectors
    Rabbit, 9" dish & cover—Milk Glass Collectors
    Squirrel with Acorn base & cover—Brodak
    Swan, 5" dish cover—Fenton
    Turkey, 5" cover—Fenton
    Turkey, large base & cover—Mosser
    Turtle cover, 5"—Milk Glass Collectors
    Turtle, base & cover—Milk Glass Collectors

Dahlia (probably Dugan molds)
    Compote—AA or Castle
    Goblet—Mosser

Daisy & Button, No. 22 (copies of patterns by many companies that made Daisy & Button)
    Anvil ash tray—AA or Castle
    Ash tray and nappy, square—AA or Castle
    Base & cover, three toed—Fenton
    Basket—AA or Castle
    Boat-shaped dish—AA or Castle
    Bone tray—Gibson
    Bowl, 4" footed—Fenton
    Bowl, 4" oval toed—Fenton
    Bowl, 6" oval—AA or Castle
    Bowl, star—Fenton
    Butter cover—AA or Castle
    Butter tub, mini—Fenton
    Candle holder—Unknown
    Candy jar & cover, 8"—AA or Castle
    Canoe, 11-1/2"—AA or Castle
    Cart ash tray—AA or Castle
    Cart, large—AA or Castle
    Cart, medium four wheeled—AA or Castle
    Cheese & cover—Fenton
    Compote, 6" square—Fenton
    Compote & cover, 4-1/2" round—Fenton
    Compote base, 4"—Fenton
    Cream, square—Fenton
    Cruet—AA or Castle
    Fan dish—Fenton
    Fan toothpick—Unknown
    Fan tray, large—Fenton
    Finger bowl, 5"—Unknown
    Flatiron base & cover—Alladin Mantle
    Font, pear, blown—Fenton
    Goblet—Fenton
    Honey base, round, 5"—Fenton
    Horseshoe top & base—AA or Castle
    Nappy or pickle, handled—AA or Castle
    Planter, 6" deep, four toed—AA or Castle
    Planter, small wall—AA or Castle
    Plate—Fenton
    Plate, 10"—AA or Castle
    Relish tray, 8" three part—Duck Soup
    Rose bowl, 5"—Fenton
    Salt dip—Unknown
    Salt shaker—Fenton
    Sauce (two)—Fenton
    Sauce, star—Fenton
    Sauce, 5" square—Fenton
    Shell footed bowl—Fenton
    Shell footed bowl, large—AA or Castle
    Sherbet, square—Fenton
    Shoe—Unknown
    Skillet—AA or Castle
    Slipper—Unknown
    Slipper, 4"—Fenton
    Sleigh, large—Mosser
    Sleigh, small—Fenton

Spoon—Rosso
Sugar, small cube—AA or Castle
Sugar & cover—Fenton
Toothpick—Unknown
Tray, 8" round—Fenton
Triangle toothpick—Unknown
Triangle tray—Fenton
Tumbler—Fenton
Wall planter—AA or Castle
Water pitcher—AA or Castle
Wine—Fenton

Daisy & Fern (copy of Northwood's Daisy & Fern)
Seven optic molds—Mosser

Daisy Cube (copy of Log & Star pattern by Bellaire Goblet Co., Findlay, Ohio)
Goblet—Fenton
Toy lamp base—Fenton

Dolphin compote—Possibly a Northwood/Dugan mold—unknown

Double Wedding Ring, No. 11 (original Wright pattern)
Compote & cover—Fenton
Goblet—Fenton
Plate, 8"—Wilkerson
Salt dip—Gibson
Sherbet & cover—Fenton
Toothpick—Fenton

Tumbler, short stemmed—Wilkerson
Wine—Fenton

Drape & Star
Bowl—Fenton
Bowl, small—Fenton

Dugan Diamonds
Sauce, small footed—Fenton

Embossed Rose (original Wright pattern)
Bowl, footed—AA or Castle
Butter & cover—AA or Castle
Candy & cover—Fenton
Candy box & cover—Fenton
Font, large—Fenton
Rose bowl (two molds)—Fenton
Shade, ball, 8"—Fenton
Shade, half, 10"—Fenton
Triangle fairy lamp—Fenton

Epergne holder—Fenton

Eye Dot & Daisy optic mold—Fenton

Eye Winker, No. 25 (copy of old Dalzell, Gilmore & Leighton Genoese, a.k.a. Eyewinker, pattern) All molds purchased by Mosser.
Ash tray
Bowl, footed, 7"
Bowl, oval, 5"
Butter, honey base
Compote & cover
Compote & cover, 6"
Cream
Fairy lampshade & base
Goblet
Marmalade & cover
Plate, 5"
Relish, deep, 8"
Salt dip
Salt shaker
Sauce, 4"
Sherbet & cover
Sugar & cover
Toothpick
Tumbler
Vase, 6"
Vase, 8"
Water pitcher
Wine

Fish
Mug—AA or Castle
Toothpick—AA or Castle

Floral
Base, footed—Mosser
Bowl, large—Rosso
Nappy, 6"—AA or Castle

Floral & Grape, No. 8
Tumbler—Mosser
Tumbler—AA or Castle

Flowers
Bowl—AA or Castle

Fluted
Barber bottle—AA or Castle
Cruet—Fenton

Frog
Salt dip—Unknown
Toothpick—Rottreis

Fruit
Bowl, 10" oval—AA or Castle
Goblet—Mosser

Goblets/Stemware
Acorn goblet—Brodak
Artichoke goblet—Mosser
BLOG—Fenton
Broken Column—Mosser
Cable—Brodak
Deer & Pine Tree goblet—Mosser
Diamond Quilted wine—Unknown
Feather goblet—Fenton
Frosted Ribbon goblet—Mosser
Grasshopper goblet—AA or Castle
Heron goblet—Mosser
Herringbone goblet—Brodak
Horn of Plenty goblet—Fenton
Inverted Dot goblet—Fenton
Lion egg cup—AA or Castle
Morning Glory champagne—AA or Castle
Morning Glory goblet—AA or Castle
Morning Glory goblet—Mosser
Morning Glory sherbet & cover—AA or Castle
Morning Glory wine (two molds)—Duck Soup
Nine Panel champagne—Unknown
Ribbed Palm goblet—AA or Castle
Rose Sprig goblet—Mosser
Star & Fan goblet—Fenton
Thousand Eye goblet—Fenton
Twelve Panel sherbet—Fenton
Two Panel goblet—Unknown
Wheat & Barley goblet—AA or Castle

God & Home, No. 1776 (original Dugan molds)
Pitcher & tumbler—Unknown

Grape, No. 4
Ball shade—Fenton
Decanter—Fenton
Shaving mug—AA or Castle
Stopper—Fenton

Grape & Fruit (No. 805)
Nappy, 10"—AA or Castle

Grape Delight
Bowl, 6" toed—AA or Castle

Grape Lattice (No. 12)
Tumbler—AA or Castle

Hand vase—AA or Castle

Harvest Flower
Pitcher & Tumbler—Mosser

Heavy Iris (original Dugan pattern)
Pitcher & cup—Fenton

Hobnail, No. 33 (old motif made by many companies)
Cream—AA or Castle
Cruet—AA or Castle
Fairy lamp shade & base—Alladin Mantle
Finger bowl & cover—AA or Castle
Goblet—Brodak
Salt shaker—AA or Castle
Sugar—AA or Castle

Jersey Swirl, No. 35 (copy of old Windsor pattern) All molds purchased by Mosser.
Compote, high footed
Compote, 5" high footed
Cover
Cover, 4"
Goblet
Master salt
Plate, 10"
Salt dip
Sauce, 4" footed
Wine (two molds)

Lattice plate—Unknown

Lattice & Grape
12" jug—Gibson

Lattice & Grapevine
tall jug—Mosser

Lattice Twig

5" nappy—Wilkerson
Leaf
    Ash tray—Brodak
    Base, three part stem—Mosser
    Bowl—Wilkerson
    Plate—Rosso
    Vase—Brodak
Maize (copy of Libbey's Maize pattern)
    Candy box & cover—Alladin Mantle
    Font, 6"—Rottreis
    Font, large—Rottreis
    Shade, 10" ball & 9" bottom plate—Fenton
    Shade, 12" ball—Rottreis
    Shade, 7" half—Rottreis
    Sugar shaker—Fenton
    Tumbler—Fenton
    Vase, 7"—AA or Castle
    Vase, 9"—AA or Castle
Maple Leaf, No. 42 (copy of Northwood/Dugan's Maple Leaf pattern)
    Butter & cover—Mosser
    Compote, stemmed—Mosser
    Cream—Unknown
    Goblet—Mosser
    Spoon—Mosser
    Sugar & cover—Unknown
    Toothpick—Mosser
    Tumbler—Mosser
    Water pitcher—Mosser
Melon
    Candy base & cover—Brodak
    Relish, two handled—Unknown
    Shade, 7"—Unknown
Mirror & Rose (original Wright pattern)
    Goblet—Rottreis
    Salt shaker—Gibson
    Wine—Fenton
Moon & Star, No. 44 (copy of old Palace pattern, a.k.a. Moon & Star, by Adams)
    Candy, footed—Gibson
    Decanter—Fenton
    Decanter stopper—Fenton
    Spoon—Unknown
    Syrup jug—Unknown
    Wine (two molds)—Fenton
NOTE: All the following molds were purchased by Weishar who made the molds for Wright.
    Ash tray, 5"
    Ash tray, 8"
    Butter & cover
    Candlestick
    Candlestick, 9"
    Champagne
    Compote
    Compote, 4" (two molds)
    Compote, 6" (three molds)
    Compote, 6" low
    Compote, footed, open

    Compote cover
    Compote cover, 6"
    Cover (three molds)
    Cover, 8"
    Cruet
    Egg cup
    Epergne cone
    Fairy lamp top
    Finger bowl
    Goblet (three molds)
    Ice tea
    Lamp base, large
    Lamp base, short
    Lamp font
    Lamp shade, mini
    Nappy, 8"
    Nappy, handled
    Pickle tray, large
    Plate, 10" round
    Plate with flared scallop
    Relish, oval
    Relish, 8" rectangular
    Salt dip
    Salt shaker
    Sherbet
    Soap dish
    Spoon
    Sugar
    Sugar shaker
    Toothpick
    Toothpick, large
    Tray, 12"
    Tumbler
    Vase, 6"
    Vase, 7"
    Water pitcher
    Wine
Panel Daisy
    Ash tray, large—AA or Castle
    Goblet—Mosser
    Relish—New Old Products
Panel Grape, No. 55 (copy of Westmoreland pattern) All molds purchased by Mosser.
    Bowl
    Bowl, 9"
    Compote & cover, 6"
    Cordial
    Cream
    Cream, small
    Cup
    Goblet
    Ice tea
    Jug
    Punch cup
    Salad plate, 8" & bowl
    Sauce, 4"
    Sherbet (two molds)
    Sugar, small
    Sugar & cover

    Tumbler
    Vase
    Wine
Plume (copy of old Adams No. 3 pattern, Plume)
    Goblet—Brodak
    Toy base and half shade—Alladin Mantle
Priscilla, No. 56 (copy of old Dalzell, Gilmore & Leighton pattern, Alexis—a.k.a. Priscilla)
    Ash tray—Wilkerson
    Compote & cover—Brodak
    Compote & cover, 4"—Brodak
    Goblet—Brodak
    Plate/nappy, 6"—Brodak
    Rose bowl—Unknown
    Sauce—Brodak
    Sauce, 4"—Fenton
    Toothpick—Brodak
    Wine—Fenton
Pump & Trough (old Northwood pattern)
    Pump—AA or Castle
    Trough (two molds)—AA or Castle
Rabbit
    Match holder (toothpick)—Unknown
Rambler Rose, No. 800 (Northwood mold)
    Jug—Mosser
    Tumbler—Unknown
Rose
    Fairy lamp—Alladin Mantle
    Fairy lamp—Unknown
Round
    Cruet—Fenton
    Font, 7"—Fenton
S Quill
    bowl—AA or Castle
S Repeat (copy of National pattern, a.k.a. S Repeat, by National/Dugan)
    Cream—AA or Castle
    Cruet—Unknown
    Cup—Unknown
    Goblet—Brodak
    Nappy, 6"—Unknown
    Sherbet—Brodak
    Toothpick—Brodak
    Wine—Brodak
Sawtooth—All molds purchased by Fenton.
    Goblet
    Ice tea, footed
    Sherbet
    Toothpick
    Wine
Scroll
    Font, small—Unknown
    Shade, ball—Fenton

Syrup jug—Fenton

Shell & Tassel (copy of Geo. Duncan & Sons pattern, Shell & Tassel)
    Compote cover, square—Fenton
    Goblet—Mosser

Sleigh
    Small with candle plunger—Mosser

Snowflake
    Optic mold, large—Mosser
    Optic mold, small—Mosser

Stipple Star, No. 59 (original Wright pattern)
    Ball shade, 8"—AA or Castle
    Compote & cover, 8"—AA or Castle
    Cover, 6"—AA or Castle
    Cream, footed—AA or Castle
    Fairy lamp base—AA or Castle
    Fairy shade—AA or Castle
    Font—AA or Castle
    Goblet—AA or Castle
    Lamp base, large—AA or Castle
    Salt dip—Mosser
    Sugar & cover—AA or Castle
    Wine—AA or Castle

Stork & Rushes, No. 78 (old Dugan pattern, original molds)
    Bowl—Unknown
    Cream—Gibson
    Mug—AA or Castle
    Nappy, 4"—AA or Castle
    Spooner—Unknown
    Sugar & cover—Gibson
    Tumbler—Fenton
    Water pitcher—Fenton

Stove
    Base & cover—Rottreis

Strawberry & Currant
    Cream—AA or Castle
    Goblet (two molds)—Mosser
    Mug—AA or Castle
    Wine—Unknown

Stump
    toothpick—Gibson

Swan
    salt dip—Rosso

Sweetheart (copy of old Dugan Victor, a.k.a. Jeweled Heart, pattern). All molds purchased by Mosser.
    Bowl
    Cream
    Goblet
    Lamp base
    Pickle boat
    Sauce
    Sugar & cover
    Toothpick
    Wine

Sweetheart & Flowers
    Compote—Mosser

Teepee
    cruet—Fenton

Thistle, No. 64 (copy of old Higbee pattern, Paneled Thistle)
    Bowl & cover, low—Brodak
    Bowl, oval—Brodak
    Bowl, 5-1/2"—Fenton
    Bowl, 7-1/2"—Unknown
    Butter & cover—Rosso
    Compote & cover, large—Brodak
    Compote & cover, small—Brodak
    Cream, large—Fenton
    Cream, small—Fenton
    Cup—Unknown
    Fairy lamp shade & base—Alladin Mantle
    Goblet (two molds)—Brodak
    Honey base & cover—Fenton
    Plate, 10"—Brodak
    Plate, round 7"—Brodak
    Plate, square—Brodak
    Relish—Brodak
    Relish, oval—Brodak
    Salt dip—Brodak
    Salt shaker—Fenton
    Sauce—Brodak
    Sauce—Fenton
    Sauce, handled with candle well plunger—Brodak
    Sherbet—Brodak
    Spoon—Rosso
    Sugar—Unknown
    Sugar & cover, large—Fenton
    Sugar & cover, small—Fenton
    Sugar shaker—Fenton
    Toothpick—Fenton
    Tumbler—Brodak
    Vase—Fenton
    Water pitcher—Brodak

Three Face, No. 65 (copy of Geo. Duncan & Sons pattern, Three Face)
    Claret—AA or Castle
    Compote & cover, 6" (two molds)—AA or Castle
    Compote base, low—AA or Castle
    Cream—AA or Castle
    Goblet—AA or Castle
    Lamp base & font—Alladin Mantle
    Salt dip—Rosso
    Salt shaker—AA or Castle
    Sherbet & cover—AA or Castle
    Spooner—AA or Castle
    Sugar—AA or Castle
    Sugar shaker—AA or Castle

Tree of Life, No. 60 (old motif, but new molds by Wright)
    Compote & cover, 4"—Fenton
    Goblet—Brodak
    Nappy, 5"—Brodak
    Relish, fan shape, 7"—Brodak
    Sauce, three toed, 4"—Brodak
    Wine—Brodak

Twig
    Tumbler—Brodak
    Vase, 3"—Fenton

Vine
    Cruet—Fenton
    Salt dip—Gibson

Violin
    Ash tray—Rottreis
    Base & cover—Alladin Mantle

Westward Ho, No. 66 (copy of Gillinder's pattern, Westward Ho)
NOTE: All molds purchased by AA or Castle.
    Butter & cover
    Celery
    Compote & cover, 6"
    Compote & cover, low oval, 7"
    Compote & cover, round, 5"
    Cream
    Goblet
    Sherbet & cover
    Sugar & cover
    Tumbler
    Wine

Wildflower, No. 67 (copy of Adams No. 140 pattern, a.k.a. Wildflower)
    Compote, 4"—Gibson
    Compote & cover, 6"—Fenton
    Cream—AA or Castle
    Goblet—Fenton
    Salt dip, crescent—Gibson
    Salt dip, rectangular—Unknown
    Stick candy—Gibson
    Sugar—AA or Castle
    Sugar—Unknown
    Vase, 6"—Unknown
    Wine—Fenton

Wildrose (original Wright pattern)
    Candy & cover, large, tall—AA or Castle
    Goblet (four molds)—AA or Castle
    Spooner—Mosser
    Tea—Fenton
    Wine (two molds)—Fenton

L. G. Wright Catalog Illustrations

Catalog Page from 1966—All purple slag. **Row 1:** S Toothpick 77-63, $12; Bee Hive Honey Dish 77-8, $25; 3" Hen 70-7, $30; 7" Hen 70-8, $50; **Row 2:** Atterbury Duck 70-2, $70; Cherry Scroll Compote 7-3, $18; Fish Toothpick 77-59, $20; **Row 3:** Sawtooth Goblet 77-35, $18; Cherry Cream 7-4, $22; Cherry Sugar 7-5, $22; Daisy & Button Square Ash Tray 22-3, $12.

Page from 1967 Catalog—Dark Blue & Dark Blue Satin. **Row 1:** 5" Hen Satin 80-7, $28; 5" Rooster Satin 80-12, $30; 7" Hen Satin 70-8, $45; 7" Hen Plain 70-8, $40; 5" Hen 80-7, $25; **Row 2:** 5" Swan Satin 80-14, $20; 5" Turtle Satin 80-16, $35; 5" Owl Satin 80-10, $35; 5" Owl Plain 80-10, $30; 5" Rooster 80-12, $28; **Row 3:** 5" Bird Satin 80-1, $20; 5" Hen Satin 80-7, $28; 5" Horse 80-8, $30; 5" Lamb 80-9, $30; 5" Cow 80-3, $30; **Row 4:** 5" Bird 80-1, $18; 5" Frog 80-6, $30; 5" Turtle 80-16, $30; 5" Swan 80-14, $18; 5" Rabbit 80-11, $30.

Row 1: 5" Rabbit 80-11, $25, $20, $25; 5" Duck 80-5, $25, $20, $35; **Row 2:** 5" Cow 80-3, $20, $25, $25; 5" Turtle 80-16, $30, $25, $25, $35, $20; **Row 3:** 5" Owl 80-10, $25, $20; 5" Rooster 80-12, $30, $25, $25, $20, $35; **Row 4:** 5" Frog 80-6, $25, $20, $30; 5" Hen 80-7, $20, $30, $35, $25, $25; **Row 5:** 5" Bird 80-1, $15, $18, $25; 5" Swan 80-14, $18, $15, $15; **Row 6:** 5" Horse 80-8, $25, $20; 5" Lamb 80-9, $25, $20; 5" Turkey 80-15, $25, $20, $35, $25.

L. G. Wright reproduction barber bottles do not have ground pontils. **Row 1:** Hobnail Barber Bottle 33-1, $85 Satin, $75, $70 Satin, $65, $85 Satin, $75; **Row 2:** Atterbury Duck 70-2, $125, $75, $125; **Row 3:** Large Turtle 70-12, $75; 7" Hen on Nest 70-8, $80; Acorn-Squirrel, $45; 7" Hen on Nest 70-8, $80.

Row 1: 5" Turkey on Nest 80-15, $35, $25, $20; **Row 2:** 5" Rooster on Nest 80-12, $40; 5" Hen on Nest 80-7, $40; 5" Rooster on Nest 80-12, $25; 5" Hen on Nest 80-7, $25; **Row 3:** 5" Owl on Nest 80-10, $22, $25, $20; 5" Swan on Nest 80-14, $15; **Row 4:** 5" Rooster on Nest 80-12, $35; 5" Hen on Nest 80-7, $35; 5" Rooster on Nest 80-12, $20; 5" Hen on Nest 80-7, $20; **Row 5:** 5" Bird on Nest 80-1, $25, $35, $15, $18; **Row 6:** 6-1/2" Duck 80-5, $60, $20, $25, $35.

All purple slag: Large Turkey 70-17, $100; Milk Glass with Carnival Head, $60; Milk Glass, $100; Carnival, $100; Carnival with Milk Glass Head: 5" Turkey 80-15, $50; 5" Rooster 80-12, $45; 5" Turtle 18-16, $50; 5" Hen 80-7, $40; Ferdinand Mustard Jar 77-46, $65; 5" Owl 80-10, $40; 5" Lamb 80-9, $50; 5" Cat 80-2, $50; 5" Horse 80-8, $50; 5" Cow 80-3, $50; 5" Swan 80-14, $40.

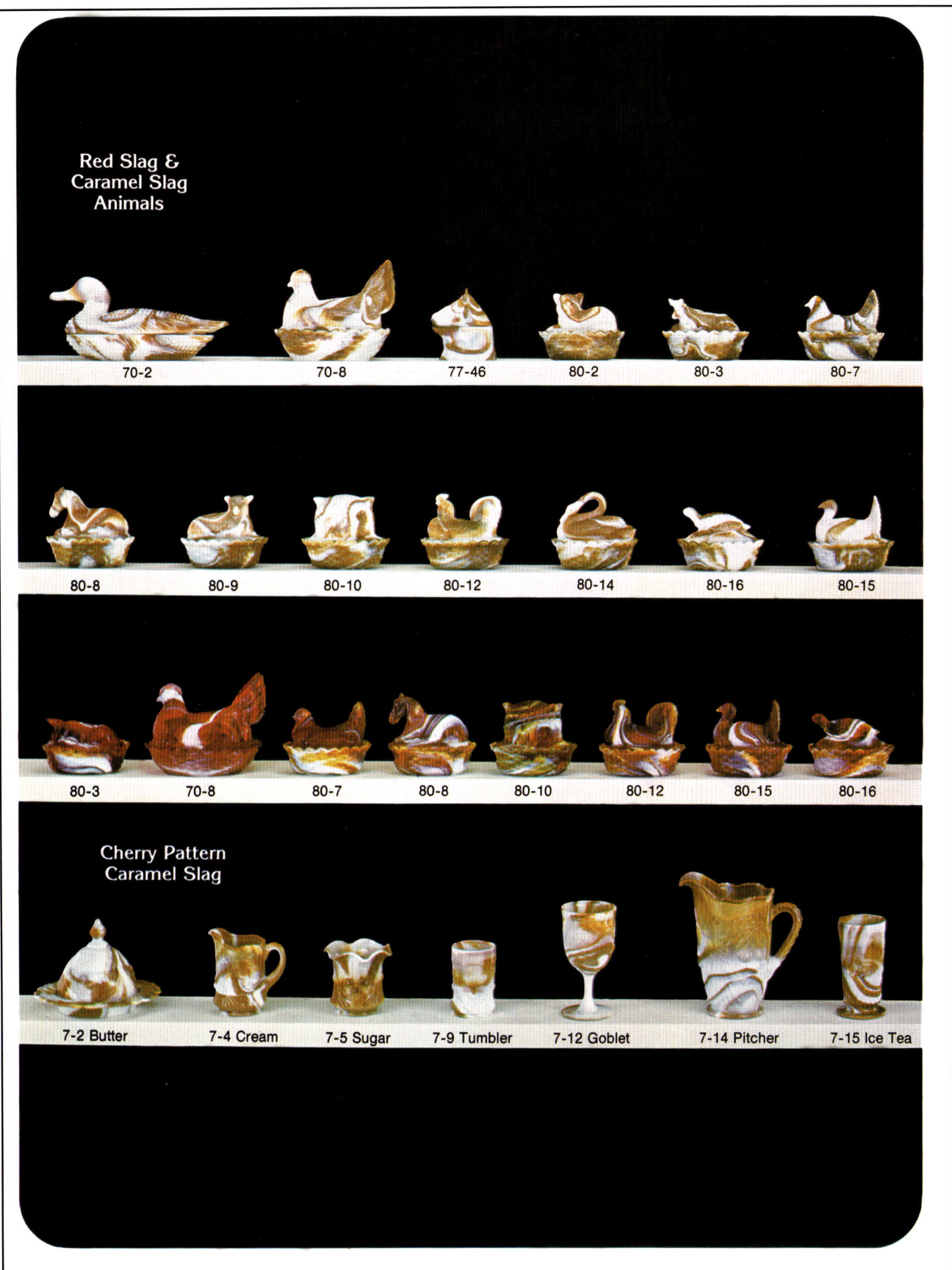

Red Slag and Caramel Slag: **Row 1:** Atterbury Duck 70-2, $80; 7" Hen 70-8, $45; Ferdinand Mustard Jar 77-46, $50; 5" Cat 80-2, $40; 5" Cow 80-3, $40; 5" Hen 80-7, $35; **Row 2:** 5" Horse 80-8, $40; 5" Lamb 80-9, $40; 5" Owl 80-10, $35; 5" Rooster 80-12, $35; 5" Swan 80-14, $35; 5" Turtle 80-16, $40; 5" Turkey 80-15, $40; **Row 3:** 5" Cow 80-3, $65; 7" Hen 70-8, $70; 5" Hen 80-7, $50; 5" Horse 80-8, $65; 5" Owl 80-10, $50; 5" Rooster 80-12, $50; 5" Turkey 80-15, $65; 5" Turtle 80-16, $65; **Row 4:** All Cherry: Butter 7-2, $25; Cream 7-4, $18; Sugar 7-5, $18; Tumbler 7-9, $15; Goblet 7-12, $15; Pitcher 7-14, $30; Ice Tea 7-15, $18.

Catalog Page from 1984. **Row 1:** God & Home Tumbler 1776-T, $20; God & Home Water Pitcher 1776-P, $95; 5" Cat 80-2, $45; 5" Hen 80-7, $42; 5" Rooster 80-12, $42; **Row 2:** 5" Cow 80-3, $45; 5" Owl 80-10, $42; 5" Turkey 80-15, $45; 5" Horse 80-8, $45; Atterbury Duck 70-2, $90; **Row 3:** Frog Candy 77-127, $60; Rabbit 77-128, $65; 7" Hen 70-8, $55; Thistle Plate 64-37, $20; **Row 4:** Maple Leaf: Toothpick 42-8, $20; Sugar & Cover 42-2, $30; Cream 42-1, $25; Spoon 42-7, $25; Butter & Cover 42-3, $45; **Row 5:** Maple Leaf: Tumbler 42-5, $20; Pitcher 42-6, $65; Compote 42-4, $35; Frog Candy 77-127, $60; 7" Hen 70-8, $55.

Row 1: Thumbprint Short Vase, $45; Opal Eye Dot Vase, $85; Fern Vase, $145; Opal Swirl Vase, $125; Thumbprint Vase, $95; Opal Honeycomb Vase, $135; Small Honeycomb Vase, $85; Vase, $35;
Row 2: Small Pitchers: Thumbprint, $75; Quilt, $75; Opal Swirl, $95; Rib, $75; Opal Honeycomb, $95; Opal Swirl, $75; **Row 3:** Water Pitchers, various shaped tops: Opal Eye Dot, $125; Fern, $165; Opal Thumbprint, $125; Fern, $165; Opal Swirl, $165; Fern, $225; **Row 4:** Water Pitchers, crimped tops: Opal Honeycomb, $165; Quilt, $125; Opal Honeycomb, $185; Thumbprint, $125; Swirl, $125; Opal Dot, $165.

Row 1: Fern Small Vase, $75; Opal Honeycomb Small Vase, $65; Swirl Small Vase, $55; Hobnail Plate & Fingerbowl, $25; Opal Eye Dot Plate & Fingerbowl, $125; Opal Hobnail Plate and Fingerbowl, $85; Thumbprint Small Vase, $55; Opal Swirl Small Vase, $65; Opal Eye Dot Small Vase, $75; **Row 2:** Fingerbowls: Opal Dot, $50; Fern, $50; Opal Swirl, $50; Thumbprint, $35; Opal Swirl, $45; Opal Dot, $45; Fern, $60; Thumbprint, $25; Honeycomb, $50, $45, $50; **Row 3:** Tumblers: Opal Swirl, $35; Fern, $35, $50; Opal Dot, $30; Thumbprint, $25; Opal Honeycomb, $35, $30; Thumbprint Juice, $20; Opal Swirl, $30; Thumbprint, $20; Opal Eye Dot, $35, $40; Thumbprint, $20; Opal Dot, $35; **Row 4:** Ice Teas: Opal Swirl, $35; Fern, $45; Opal Swirl, $40; Opal Dot, $35. Sugar Shakers: Opal Swirl, $150; Thumbprint, $95; Fern, $195; Swirl, $95; Opal Dot, $150. Ice Teas: Opal Dot, $40; Thumbprint, $25; Honeycomb, $40, $35.

Row 1: Thumbprint Sugar, $65; Thumbprint Cream, $65; Honeycomb Sugar, $85; Honeycomb Cream, $85; Honeycomb Cream, Crimped Top, $95; Honeycomb Sugar, Crimped Top, $95; Quilt Sugar, Square Top, $65; Quilt Cream, Square Top, $65; **Row 2:** Tall Creams: Honeycomb, $95; Fern, $85; Quilt, $55; Fern, $105; Honeycomb, $85; Thumbprint, $55; Opal Lattice, $95; Opal Dot, $85, $95; Opal Swirl, $85, $95; Opal Eye Dot, $105; **Row 3:** Cruets: Thumbprint, $75; Opal Swirl, $110; Fern, $150; Honeycomb, $120, $145; Fern, $150; Opal Eye Dot, $175; Thumbprint, $75; Opal Eye Dot, $175; Opal Swirl, $120; Swirl, $75; Opal Dot, $125; Thumbprint, $75; Opal Eye Dot, $150; Quilt, $80; Thumbprint, $75; **Row 4:** Barber Bottles: Opal Rib, $175; Thumbprint, $130; Opal Rib, $200; Rib, $130; Opal Swirl, $225, $175; Thumbprint, $130; Fern, $225, $275; Thumbprint, $130; Opal Eye Dot, $250, $225.

Row 1: Moss Rose: Small Vase, $85; Finger bowl, $55; Tumbler, $50; Pitcher, $200; Small Rose Bowl, $80; Large Rose Bowl, $95; Vase, $110. **Row 2:** Moss Rose: Tall Vase, $150; Lamp Shade, $50; Lamp Globe, $50; Lamp Shade, $50; Tall Vase, $150. **Row 3:** Honeycomb Luster, $375; Moss Rose Cruet, $95; Large Lamp Dome, $50; Cruet, $95; Fern Luster, $475.

Row 1: Apothecary Jars: Short Thumbprint, $95; Medium Thumbprint, $135; Tall Thumbprint, $165; Large Fern Satin, $325; Small Fern Satin, $300; **Row 2:** Apothecary Jars: Short Fern, $225; Medium Fern, $250; Tall Fern, $275; Large Fern, $300; Medium Fern, $275; **Row 3:** Medium Thumbprint, $125; Tall Thumbprint, $155.

Page from 1967 Catalog. **Row 1:** Water Pitchers: Opal Dot 84-3, $175; Thumbprint 84-1, $125; Opal Swirl 84-4, $165; Fern 84-2, $165, $225; Opal Swirl 84-4, $165; **Row 2:** Water Pitchers: Opal Thumbprint, $165; Thumbprint, $95; Honeycomb 84-5, $185, $165; Thumbprint, $65; **Row 3:** Swirl Milk Pitcher 85-11, $75; Rib Milk Pitcher 85-9, $75; Thumbprint Large Oval Apothecary Jar 87-1, $65, $125; Thumbprint Medium Oval Apothecary Jar 86-1, $155; Thumbprint Milk Pitcher 85-1, $75; **Row 4:** Milk Pitchers: Honeycomb, $95; Fern 85-2, $115; Opal Swirl 85-4, $95; Rib 85-9, $65; Thumbprint 85-1, $55; Quilt 85-7, $75.

Row 1: Tall Creams: Opal Eye Dot Satin 909-6, $125; Opal Eye Dot 909-6, $95; Opal Swirl Syrup, $225; Honeycomb Syrup, $225; Fern Syrup, $275; Thumbprint Pickle Jar 98-1, $65; Stars & Stripes Tall Cream, $150; Fern Tall Cream 90-2, $105; **Row 2:** Tall Creams: Opal Dot 90-3, $95, $85; Honeycomb 90-5, $95; Opal Swirl 90-4, $86, $95; Thumbprint, $55; Opal Lattice, $95; Quilt, $55; **Row 3:** Thumbprint Short Sugar 91-1, $65; Thumbprint Short Cream 91-1, $65; Quilt Sugar, $65; Quilt Cream, $65. Ice Teas: Opal Dot, $40; Thumbprint, $10; Thumbprint, $25; Opal Swirl, $40; Fern Satin, $50; **Row 4:** Tumblers: Opal Eye Dot 97-1, $40; Fern 97-2, $50, $50; Opal Dot 97-3, $30, $35; Thumbprint 97-1, $25, $10, $15; Stars & Stripes, $65, $55; Thumbprint 91-1, $15, $15; **Row 5:** Thumbprint Finger Bowl, $35, $20. Sugar Shakers: Fern 96-2, $150; Opal Swirl 96-4, $120; Opal Dot 96-3, $150, $125; Thumbprint 96-1, $95. Tumblers: Opal Swirl 97-4, $30, $35; Honeycomb 97-5, $30, $35; **Row 6:** Finger Bowls: Opal Dot, $50, $45; Thumbprint, $25, $25; Honeycomb Satin, $60; Honeycomb, $45; Opal Swirl, $50; Fern, $60.

Row 1: Barber Bottles: Fern 88-2, $225, $275, $275; Fern Satin 88-2, $295; Opal Eye Dot Satin 88-6, $295; Opal Eye Dot 88-6, $225, $250; Opal Swirl Satin 88-4, $250; Opal Swirl 88-4, $175, $225; **Row 2:** Barber Bottles: Opal Rib 88-10, $200, $200, $175; Opal Rib Satin 88-10, $225; Thumbprint 89-1, $130; Quilt, $130; Cruets: Quilt Fluted Vine, $80; S 77-12, $30, $45, $45; **Row 3:** Honeycomb Oval Cruet 94-5 Satin, $160, $120; Thumbprint Oval Cruet 94-1, $75; Opal Dot Oval Cruet 94-3, $135; Fluted Thumbprint Cruet 93-1, $75; Thumbprint Fluted Vine Cruet 93-1, $75; Fluted Opal Eye Dot Cruet 92-6 (2), $160, $195; Thumbprint Round Cruet 95-1, $75; Opal Dot Round Cruet 95-3, $160; **Row 4:** Fern Round Cruet 95-2, $150; Fern Round Cruet Satin 95-2, $185; Fern Oval Cruet 94-2, $150; Fern Oval Cruet 94-2, $165; Thumbprint Round Cruet, $50, $45, $30; Swirl Round Cruet 95-4, $75; Opal Swirl Round Cruet 95-4, $120; Opal Swirl Oval Cruet, $160.

Row 1: 7" Hobnail Fairy Light 33-6, $75; Daisy & Cube Miniature Lamp 45-A, $90; Daisy & Cube Miniature Lamp 45-G, $125; Embossed Rose Triangle Fairy Light 77-47A, $80; Daisy & Cube Miniature Lamp 45-B, $135; Daisy & Cube Miniature Lamp 45-AR, $195; Hobnail Fairy Lamp 33-B, $85; **Row 2:** Embossed Rose Fairy Lights: 34-A 7", $75; 34-R, $150; Triangle 77-47G, $95; 34-B, $95; 34-G, $85; **Row 3:** Hobnail 7" Fairy Light 33-A, $55; Thumbprint Miniature Lamp 36-1, $135; 10" Opal Eye Dot Miniature Lamp 11-6, $200; Thumbprint Miniature Lamp 11-1, $145; Opal Dot Miniature Lamp 10-6, $190; Hobnail Fairy Light 33-R, $140; **Row 4:** Miniature Lamps: 9" Opal Honeycomb 10-5, $200; Swirl 10-11, $145; Opal Swirl 11-4, $190; Opal Dot 11-3, $200; Opal Swirl 10-4, $180; Opal Dot 10-3, $190.

Row 1: Cranberry Barber Bottles: Fern 88-2, $275; Opal Swirl 88-4, $225; Opal Eye Dot 88-6, $250; Opal Rib 88-10, $200; Thumbprint 89-1, $130. Cranberry Syrup Pitchers: Opal Swirl 86A-4, $225; Honeycomb 86A-5, $225; Fern 86A-2, $275. **Row 2:** Cranberry Sugar Shakers: Thumbprint 86-1, $95; Opal Dot 86-3, $150; Fern 86-2, $195; Opal Swirl 86-4, $150. Cranberry Cruets: Round Fern 85-2, $165; Round Opal Dot 85-3, $125; Round Thumbprint 95-1, $75; **Row 3:** Thumbprint Cranberry Short Cream & Sugar Set 91-1, $65 each. Cranberry Cruets: Oval Thumbprint 94-1, $75; Fluted Thumbprint 92-1, $75; Oval Fern 94-2, $165; **Row 4:** Cranberry Tumblers: Opal Dot 97-3, $35; Thumbprint 97-1, $25; Fern 97-2, $50; Opal Swirl 97-4, $35; Honeycomb 97-5, $35; Opal Eye Dot 97-6, $40; Stars & Stripes 97-8, $75.

Right to left: Row 1: Cranberry Water Pitchers: Opal Dot 84-3, $175; Fern 84-2, $225; Opal Swirl 84-4, $175; Opal Honeycomb 84-5, $185; **Row 2:** Cranberry Water Pitcher: Thumbprint 84-1, $125. Cranberry Milk Pitchers: Fern, $115; Opal Dot, $100; **Row 3:** Cranberry Tall Creams: Fern 90-2, $105; Opal Honeycomb 90-5, $95; Opal Swirl 90-4, $95. Cranberry Milk Pitchers: Opal Honeycomb, $95; Opal Swirl, $95; **Row 4:** Cranberry Tall Creams: Opal Dot 90-3, $95; Thumbprint 90-1, $55. Cranberry Milk Pitcher: Thumbprint, $75.

Row 1: Syrups: Honeycomb 96A-5, $225; Fern 96A-2, $275; Opal Swirl 96A-4, $225. Sugar Shakers: Opal Dot 96-3, $150; Thumbprint 96-1, $95; Opal Swirl 96-4, $150; Fern 96-2, $195; **Row 2:** Barber Bottles: Opal Eye Dot 88-6, $250; Fern 88-2, $275; Opal Rib 88-10, $200. Cruets: Fern Round 95-2, $165; Thumbprint 95-1, $75; Opal Dot 95-3, $125; Thumbprint 94-1, $75; Fluted Thumbprint 92-1, $75; **Row 3:** Barber Bottles: Thumbprint 89-1, $130; Fern 88-2, $275; Opal Swirl 88-4, $225. Pickle Casters in Frames: Daisy & Button 22-36-5, $95, $125, $195; **Row 4:** Pickle Casters in Frames: Fern 98-2-5, $275; Thumbprint 98-1-5, $185; Moss Rose 99-40-5, $150; Opal Dot 98-3-5, $245; Opal Swirl 98-4-5, $225.

Page from 1980 Supplement Catalog. Blue Fern Biscuit Jar, $250; Vaseline Fern Biscuit Jar 98-9, $295; Cranberry Christmas Snowflake Tumbler 97-9, $80; Cranberry Christmas Snowflake Water Pitcher 84-6, $325.

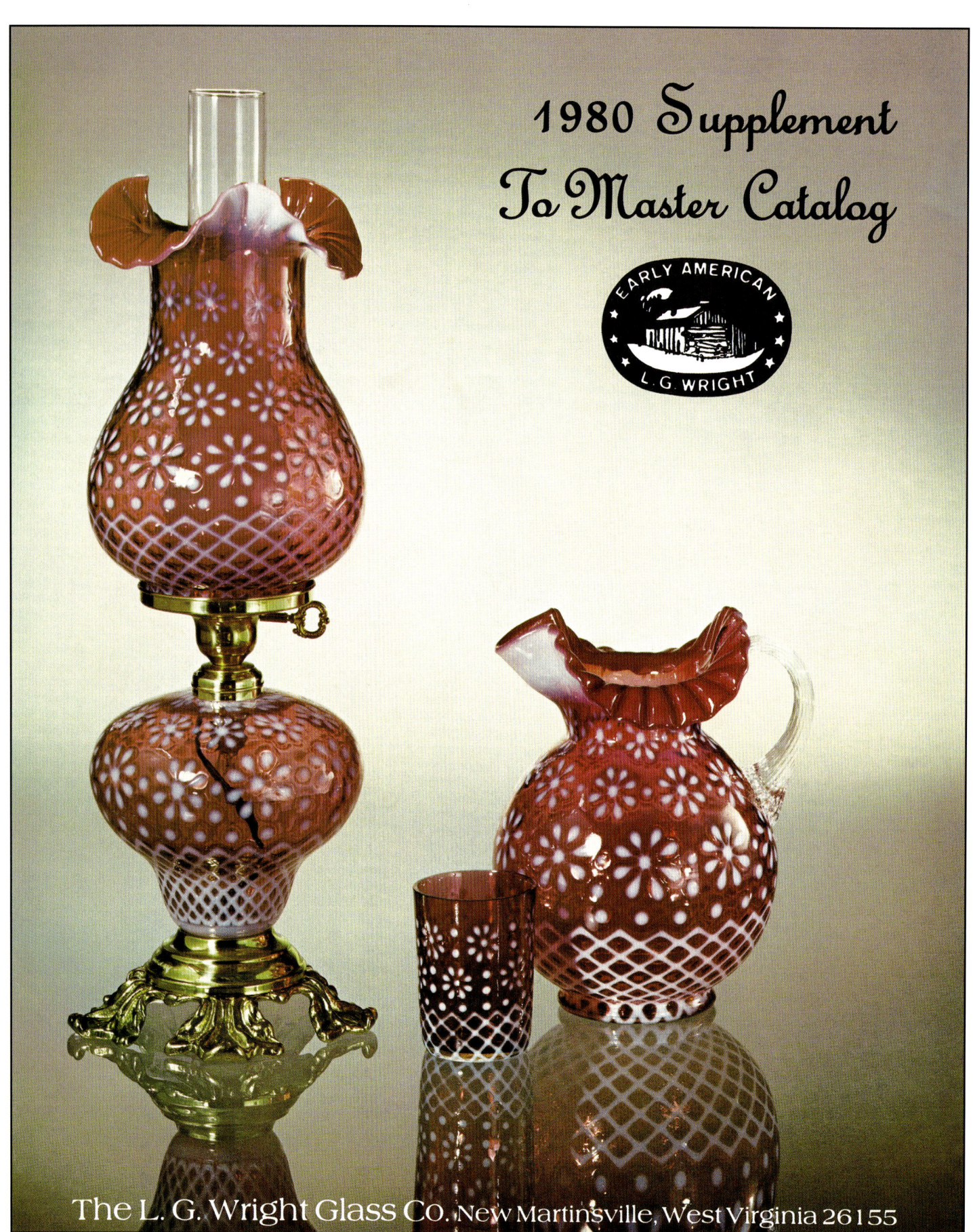

Cover of 1980 Supplement Catalog. Cranberry Christmas Snowflake Lamp, $400; Tumbler, $80; Water Pitcher, $325.

All Vaseline Opalescent, made ca. 1965. **Row 1:** Beaded Small Footed Ivy Bowl 3-4, $48; Daisy & Button 5" 4 Toed Candleholder 22-14, $35; Daisy & Button 5" 4 Toed Bowl 22-8, $30; Beaded 3 Piece Console Set 3-1-3, Candle, $60, Bowl, $80; **Row 2:** Opal Rib Barber Bottle 12 oz. 88-10, $200; Fern Barber Bottle 12 oz. 88-2, $275; 7" Hen on Nest 70-8, $125; Cherry Sugar 7-4, $35; Cherry Cream 7-5, $45; Round Fern Cruet 8 oz. 95-2, $185; Oval Fern Cruet 8 oz. 94-2, $185; **Row 3:** Moon & Star Wine 2 oz. 44-42, $45; Daisy & Button 4" Square Sauce 22-50, $25; Daisy & Button Thumbprint Panel Goblet 8 oz. 22-30, $60; Daisy & Button Thumbprint Panel Wine 4 oz. 22-69, $40; Daisy & Button Sugar 22-23, $30; Daisy & Button Cream 22-24, $35; Daisy & Button Fan Toothpick 4" 22-62, $45; Daisy & Button Round Toothpick 2-1/2" 22-63, $30; **Row 4:** Strawberry & Currant Goblet 8 oz. 77-36, $45; Panel Grape Goblet 8 oz. 55-7, $55; Moon & Star goblet, 9 oz. 44-22, $65; Wildflower Goblet 8 oz. 67-5, $45; Wildflower Wine 2 oz. 67-12, $30; Strawberry & Currant Crimpt (**Note: L.G. Wright used this spelling for "crimped".**) Footed Compote 6-1/2" 72-5, $45; Beaded Small Footed Crimpt Compote 3-2, $55; **Row 5:** Beaded Large Footed Ivy Bowl 3-5, $65; Beaded Large Footed Crimpt Compote 3-3, $60; Daisy & Button Plate 10" 22-39, $50; Fern Tumbler 8 oz. 97-2, $50; Fern Water Pitcher 2-1/2 qt. 84-2, $250.

Row 1: Pickle Casters in Frames: Daisy & Button 22-36-103, $95, $195, $175, $125; Moss Rose 99-40-404, $150; **Row 2:** Pickle Casters in Frames: Thumbprint 98-1-404, $185; Opal Swirl 98-4-404, $225; Opal Dot 98-3-404, $245; Fern 98-2-4-4, $275; Mirror & Rose 77-108-404, $190; **Row 3:** Pickle Casters in Frames: Mirror & Rose 77-108-103, $115, $190, $220; Opal Swirl 98-4-103, $225; Thumbprint 98-1-103, $185; **Row 4:** Brides Baskets: 11" Crimpt Bowl, Toy Rose 108-22-100-9, $120; 11" Crimpt Bowl, Rose of Yesteryear 115-18-117, $95; 11" Crimpt Bowl, Rose of Yesteryear 113-18 without frame, $40.

All Vaseline Opalescent. **Row 1:** Rib Barber Bottle 88-10, $200; Fern Barber Bottle Satin 88-2, $295; Fern Tumbler Satin 97-2, $60; Fern Water Pitcher, $250; Fern Tumbler 97-2, $50; Fern Oval Cruet 94-2, $185; Fern Round Cruet 95-2, $185; **Row 2:** Beaded Small Ivy Bowl 3-4, $48; Strawberry & Currant Compote 72-5, $45; Daisy & Button 10" 4 Toed Bowl 22-7, $120; Corn Vase 75-1, $135; Jersey Swirl Compote 35-4, $50; **Row 3:** Daisy & Button Toothpick 22-63, $30; Daisy & Button Square Sauce 22-50, $25; Daisy & Button 5" Oval 4 Toed Bowl 22-8, $30; Daisy & Button 4" Covered Compote 22-17, $55; Dolphin Compote 72-3, $50; Beaded Crimpt Small Compote 3-2, $55.

All Vaseline Opalescent. **Top:** Moon & Star Decanter 44-18, $195; Moon & Star Wine 44-42, $45; Fern Lamp 17" 100-5, $300; Fern Lamp 21" 100-4, $375; **Bottom:** Fern Tumbler 100-2, $50; Fern Ice Tea 100-3, $65; Fern Water Pitcher 100-1, $250.

All Blue Opal. **Row 1:** All Cherry: 10" Oval Bowl 7-16, $65; Goblet 7-12, $30; Ice Tea 7-15, $25; Water Pitcher 7-14, $95; **Row 2:** All Cherry: 5" Oval Bowl 7-17, $24; Sugar 7-5, $24; Cream 7-4, $28; Tumbler 7-9, $20; **Row 3:** Corn Vase 77-121, $85; Cherry Toothpick 7-8, $25; Cherry Butter 7-2, $65; **Row 4:** Hen on Nest 7" 7-8, $85; **Row 5:** Pump & Trough 77-95, 96, Pump, $58, Trough, $25; Dahlia Tumbler 2-2, $20; Dahlia Water Pitcher 2-1, $95.

All Vaseline Fern. **Row 1:** Pickle Jar with Cover 98-2, $220; Pickle Jar with Plain Frame 98-2-103, $295; Milk Pitcher 85-2, $135; Tall Cream 90-2, $125; Hurricane Lamp 725, $165; **Row 2:** Round Barber Bottle 89-2, $275; Fluted Barber Bottle 88-2, $275; Water Pitcher 84-2, $250; Tumbler 97-2, $50; Ice Tea 100-3, $65; Syrup Pitcher 96A-2, $295; **Row 3:** Round Cruet 95-2, $185; Wedding Bowl 11" 9808, $125; Sugar Shaker 96-2, $215; **Row 4:** Oval Cruet 94-2, $185; Small Rose Bowl 98-6, $140; Large Rose Bowl 98-7, $165.

Page from 1981 Supplement Catalog. **Top:** Opal Eye Dot & Daisy Tumbler, $125; Opal Eye Dot & Daisy Water Pitcher, $395; Fern Candy Box, $275; **Middle:** Fern Large Basket 98-14, $220; Fern Small Basket (blue) 98-16, $185; **Bottom:** Fern Large Basket 98-14, $250; Fern Candy Box 98-10, $325; Fern Small Basket (vaseline) 98-16, $220. Christmas Snowflake in Cobalt: Small Basket 98-16, $250; Small Rose Bowl 98-6, $175.

Blue Fern

All Blue Fern. **Row 1:** Hurricane Lamp 725, $145; Round Barber Bottle 89-2, $225; Fluted Barber Bottle 88-2, $225; Pickle Jar Frame 98-2-404, $275; Water Pitcher 84-2, $165; **Row 2:** Milk Pitcher 85-2, $95; 11" Wedding Bowl 98-8, $85; Tumbler 97-2, $35; **Row 3:** Large Rose Bowl 98-7, $145; Small Rose Bowl 98-6, $120; Oval Cruet 94-2, $150; Pickle Jar with cover 98-2, $185; **Row 4:** Syrup Pitcher 96A-2, $250; Sugar Shaker 96-2, $150; Round Cruet 95-2, $150; Tall Cream 90-2, $85.

All Cobalt Christmas Snowflake. **Row 1:** Round Barber Bottle 89-3, $295; Milk Pitcher 85-12, $200; Tumbler 97-10, $125; Water Pitcher 84-7, $345; **Row 2:** Spooner 98-6, $95; Oval Cruet 94-6, $225; Tall Cream 90-14, $175; Syrup Pitcher 96A-6, $295; **Row 3:** Wedding Bowl 98-11, $175; Rose Bowl 98-9, $225; Sugar Shaker 96-12, $225.

MAPLE LEAF CARNIVAL GLASS
Made From Original Moulds

42-3 Covered Butter

42-5 Tumbler

42-7 Spooner

42-2 Covered Sugar

42-1 Cream

All Maple Leaf: Covered Butter 42-3, $95; Tumbler 42-5, $20; Spoon 42-7, $30; Covered Sugar 42-2, $45; Cream 42-1, $35.

Top: Red Primrose Lamp 1006, $85; Red Primrose Vase 99-112, $25; Red Primrose Lamp 1002, $105; Red Primrose Lamp 1004, $105; **Bottom:** Red Primrose Candy Box 99-113, $45; Iris Tumbler 5-2, $30; Iris Water Pitcher 5-1, $125; Vaseline Fern Oil Lamp 77-124, $195; Blue Fern Oil Lamp 77-124, $165.

STORK and RUSHES
MARIGOLD

All Stork and Rushes Marigold Carnival. **Top:** Covered Sugar 78-4, $30; Cream 78-5, $25; Tumbler 78-6, $20; Water Pitcher 78-1, $75; **Middle:** Spooner 78-3, $20; **Bottom:** Sauce 78-7, $15; Berry Bowl 78-2, $35.

All Stork and Rushes Purple Carnival. **Top:** Covered Sugar 78-4, $40; Cream 78-5, $35; Tumbler 78-6, $30; Water Pitcher 78-1, $95; **Middle:** Spooner 78-3, $30; **Bottom:** Sauce 78-7, $25; Berry Bowl 78-2, $55.

PURPLE CARNIVAL

Purple Carnival. Tumblers are usually marked with a lopsided W in the bottom—made by adding a "leg" to the old Northwood N mark. **Row 1:** Rambler Rose Tumbler 800-3, $25; Grape Tumbler 920, $25; Grape & Daisy Tumbler 965, $25; Trough 77-96, $40; Pump 77-95, $85; **Row 2:** Dahlia Water Pitcher 2-1, $95; Dahlia Tumbler 2-2, $25; **Row 3:** 12" Grape & Fruit Bowl Crimpt 808-1, $65; 14" Grape & Fruit Plate, $55.

Pony 9" Plate Marigold 23-2, $55; Pony Crimped Bowl Marigold 23-1, $75; Pony 9" Plate Dark Carnival 23-2, $75; Pony Crimped Bowl Dark Carnival 23-1, $95.

Top: Grape & Cable 10" Oval Bowl 77-90, $85; Grape & Cable 6" Oval Bowl 77-111, $25; **Bottom:** Grape Nut Bowl 77-125, $48; Grape Rose Bowl 77-125, $58.

GOD and HOME WATER SET
A Rare and Treasured Pattern in Carnival Glass Once Again Produced From the Recently Discovered Original Old Moulds.

1776-WP Water Pitcher

1776-T Tumbler

Dark Carnival. God & Home Water Pitcher 1776 WP, $175; God & Home Tumbler 1776-T, $40.

Row 1: Grape Vine Lattice Tumbler 12-2, $25; Grape Vine Lattice Water Pitcher 12-1, $150; Rambler Rose Tumbler 800-3, $25; Rambler Rose Water Pitcher 800-4, $120; Floral & Grape Tumbler 8-2, $25; Floral & Grape Water Pitcher 8-1, $120; **Row 2:** Banded Grape Tumbler 9-2, $25; Banded Grape Water Pitcher 9-1, $135; Grape Wine, $20; Grape Decanter 4-1, $75; 7" Hen on Nest 70-8, $70; **Row 3:** Sweetheart Cherry 7" Round Bowl 24-1, $75; Cherry 10" Oval Bowl 7-16, $65; Cherry 5" Oval Bowl 7-17, $65.

Ice Pink

64-24 Thistle Tumbler
64-19 Thistle Water Pitcher
64-16 Thistle Spooner
64-23 Thistle Tall Sugar
64-22 Thistle Tall Cream
64-11 Thistle Butter w/cover
70-8 7" Hen on Nest

All Ice Pink Carnival. **Row 1:** Thistle Tumbler 64-24, $20; Thistle Water Pitcher 64-19, $65; Thistle Spooner 64-16, $35; **Row 2:** Thistle Tall Sugar 64-23, $30; Thistle Tall Cream 64-22, $35; **Row 3:** Thistle Butter with Cover 64-11, $55; 7" Hen on Nest 70-8, $60.

All Ice Green Carnival. **Row 1:** Maple Leaf Tumbler 42-5, $20; Maple Leaf Water Pitcher 42-6, $70; God & Home Tumbler 1776-T, $25; God & Home Water Pitcher 1776-P, $95; **Row 2:** Grape & Cable 10" Oval Bowl 77-90, $55; Grape Nut Bowl 77-126, $35; **Row 3:** Grape Rose Bowl 77-125, $35; Grape & Cable 6" Oval Bowl 77-111, $20; 7" Hen on Nest 70-8, $60.

Ruby Carnival

42-5 Maple Leaf Tumbler

42-6 Maple Leaf Water Pitcher

1776-T God & Home Tumbler

1776-P God & Home Water Pitcher

70-8 7" Hen

All Ruby Carnival. **Row 1:** Maple Leaf Tumbler 42-5, $35; Maple Leaf Water Pitcher 42-6, $110; **Row 2:** God & Home Tumbler 1776-T, $40; God & Home Water Pitcher 1776-P, $175; **Row 3:** 7" Hen 70-8, $95.

LIMITED EDITION
·1000 Sets Only·
Cobalt Carnival

Sold In Sets Only
Water Pitcher-6 tumblers

1776-P

42-6

1776-T

1776-Water Set
God & Home

42-5
Maple Leaf Water Set

God & Home

Maple Leaf Water Set

1 set God and Home (pitcher & six tumblers)	$75.00
1 set Maple Leaf (pitcher & six tumblers)	75.00

The L. G. Wright Glass Co.
New Martinsville, WV 26155

Page from 1983 Catalog. All Cobalt Carnival. God & Home Pitcher 1776-P, $175; God & Home Tumbler 1776-T, $40; Maple Leaf Water Pitcher 42-6, $110; Maple Leaf Tumbler 42-5, $35.

Amethyst Carnival

22-59	Daisy & Button Small Slipper
22-58	Daisy & Button Medium Slipper
1776T	God & Home Tumblers – 4
1776 WP	God & Home Water Pitcher
78-2	Stork & Rushes Bowl

All Amethyst Carnival. **Row 1:** God & Home Tumbler 1776 T, $40; God & Home Water Pitcher 1776 WP, $175; Stork & Rushes Bowl 78-2, $55; **Row 2:** Daisy & Button Small Slipper 22-59, $20; Daisy & Button Medium Slipper 22-58, $25; Inset: Peacock Bowl 820-3, $75.

Sweetheart and Beaded

77-11	Cream and Sugar – Crystal
	Ice Crystal
	Crystal Deco.
24-1	Sweetheart Bowl – Cobalt Carnival
	Crystal Deco.
	Ice Crystal
	Crystal
77-64	Toothpick – Crystal
	Ice Crystal
	Crystal Deco.
77-115	Fairy Lamp – Crystal Deco.
240	Sweetheart Lamp – Crystal Deco.

24-1 Sweetheart Bowl – Cobalt Carnival
3-2 Beaded Small Compote – Sparkling Ruby
3-1 Beaded Small Compote w/Candlewell – Stormy Blue

Top Photo: All Sweetheart, Gold Decoration: **Row 1:** Sweetheart Lamp 240, $70; Fairy Lamp 77-115, $65; Toothpick 77-64, $15; Bowl 24-1, $18; Covered Sugar & Cream 77-11, $25, $20; **Row 2:** All Sweetheart, Ice Crystal: Bowl 24-1, $28; Toothpick 77-64, $25; Covered Sugar & Cream 77-11, $35, $30; **Row 3:** All Sweetheart, Crystal: Covered Sugar & Cream 77-11, $20, $15; Toothpick 77-64, $12; Bowl 24-1, $15. **Bottom Photo:** Sweetheart Bowl, Cobalt Carnival 24-1, $38; Beaded Small Compote, Sparkling Ruby 3-2, $25; Beaded Small Compote with Candle well, Stormy Blue 3-1, $20.

Row 1: Moss Rose Tumbler, $55; Moss Rose Ice Tea, $65; Moss Rose Large Rose Bowl, $95; "Rose" Vase, $65; Moss Rose Vase, $75; **Row 2:** Moss Rose Syrup, $110; "Rose" Syrup, $95; "Acorn" Syrup, $95; Opal Swirl Syrup, $225; Moss Rose Pickle Jar, $110; **Row 3:** Moss Rose Small Rose Bowl, $80. Peachblow: Finger Bowl, $45; Plate, $35; Finger Bowl & Plate, $95; Satin Rose Bowl, $85.

Row 1: Moss Rose Large Rose Bowl, $95; Peachblow Large Rose Bowl, $115; Embossed Rose Vase, Satin, $90; Thumbprint Pickle Jar & Cover, $65; Moss Rose Pickle Jar & Cover, $110; Peachblow Candy Box & Cover, Satin, $165; **Row 2:** Moss Rose Round Cruet, $95; Moss Rose Fluted Vine Cruet, $95; Opal Swirl Syrup, $225; Fern Syrup, $275; Peachblow Beaded Lamp, $250; Honeycomb Syrup, $225; Moss Rose Small Rose Bowl, $80; **Row 3:** Peachblow Fairy Light, $150; "Acorn" Syrup, $95; "Rose" Syrup, $95; Moss Rose Syrup, $110; Peachblow Vase, $95; Peachblow Vase, Crimpt Top, $100; Peachblow Small Rose Bowl, $85

Row 1: Moss Rose Milk Pitcher, $200; Moss Rose Crimped Top Vase, $150; "Dogwood" Crimped Top Vase, $135. Pickle Casters in Frames: Daisy & Button, $95; Moss Rose, $150; Thumbprint, $185; **Row 2:** Moss Rose Large Rose Bowl, $115; Peachblow Large Rose Bowl, Satin, $115; Moss Rose Candy Box & Cover, $150; Peachblow Beaded Lamp, $250; "Rose" Candy Box & Cover, $130; Peachblow Candy Box & Cover, $165; "Rose" Large Rose Bowl, $85; **Row 3:** "Dogwood" Small Rose Bowl, $65; Peachblow Fairy Light, $150; "Dogwood" Candy Box & Cover, $130; Moss Rose Footed Crimped Top Vase, $85; "Rose" Candy Box & Cover, $130; "Dogwood" Large Rose Bowl, $85; Peachblow Small Rose Bowl, Satin, $85; **Row 4:** Moss Rose Small Rose Bowl, $80; Moss Rose Finger Bowl, $50; Moss Rose Cruet, $95; Peachblow Crimpt Top Vase, $100; Peachblow Vase, $95; Moss Rose Fluted Vine Cruet, $95; Moss Rose Tall Cream, $85; Moss Rose Tumbler, $50; "Floral" Small Rose Bowl, $65.

Catalog Page Ca. 1959: **Row 1:** Moss Rose Vase, $75. Cylinder Vases: Medium Grey Rose, $30; Tall Grey Rose, $40; Tall Spring Bouquet, $40; Medium Spring Bouquet, $30; Tall "Rose", $65; **Row 2:** Thumbprint Short Vase, $65; Thumbprint Tall Vase, $85; Thumbprint Bulbous Vase, $95; Fern Bulbous Vase, $150; Fern Tall Vase, $135; Fern Short Vase, $125; **Row 3:** Moss Rose Small Rose Bowl, $80; Moss Rose Large Rose Bowl, $95; "Rose" Large Rose Bowl, $85; Embossed Rose Vase, $90; Grey Rose Large Rose Bowl, $35; "Dogwood" Large Rose Bowl, $85; "Floral" Small Rose Bowl, $65.

Page from 1967 Catalog: **Row 1:** Embossed Rose Rose Bowls 75-4, $50, $35, Satin, $85, Satin, $65; **Row 2:** Maize Rose Bowls 40-2, $85, $95, Satin, $150; **Row 3:** Maize Rose Bowls 40-2 Satin, $115, Satin, $150, $175; **Row 4:** Maize Rose Bowls 40-2, $75, Satin, $195, $175.

Page from 1967 Catalog: **Row 1:** All Maize: Satin Water Pitcher 40-5, $225; 9" Vase 40-7, $110; Water Pitcher 40-5, $145; 9" Vase 40-7, $135; **Row 2:** All Maize: Tumbler 40-4, $60, $75; Sugar Shaker & Top 40-3, $135, $165; 7" Vase 40-6, $75, $105; **Row 3:** 21" Maize Lamp, $275; 13" Embossed Bird Vase 99-28, $125, $55, $95.

Row 1: Maize Rose Bowls 40-2, $195, $85, $95, $195; **Row 2:** Embossed Rose Rose Bowl 75-4, $50; Maize Candy Jar & Cover 40-1, $145, $125, $195; Maize Sugar Shaker 40-3, $155, $135; **Row 3:** Embossed Rose Satin Rose Bowl 75-4, $155, $65; Embossed Rose Vase 75-2, $165, Satin, $75, $90, Satin, $65; **Row 4:** Maize Tumbler 40-4, $75; Maize Water Pitcher 40-5, $200; Maize Tumbler 40-4, $60; Maize Water Pitcher 40-5, $145; 9" Maize Vase 40-7, $135, $95; 7" Maize Satin Vase 40-6, $105, $75; **Row 5:** Embossed Bird 13" Vase 99-27, $95; Embossed Bird 13" Vase 99-29, $55; Embossed Bird 13" Vase 99-28, $125; Maize Pickle Caster in Frame 40-8-5, $145, $155, $225.

Wedding Bowls, Decorated: **Row 1:** 13" Holland Rose, $45; **Row 2:** 13" Grape, $45; "Rose", $45; **Row 3:** 13" Toy Rose, $80; **Row 4:** 13" Wild Rose, $70; 13" Green Floral, $70; **Row 5:** 13" Rose of Yesteryear, $45; **Row 6:** 13" Violet, $70; 13" Rose of Yesteryear, $70.

Row 1: Maize Satin Rose Bowl, Metal Pedestal 40-2-3, $125; 13" Spring Flowers Wedding Bowl 102-17-1, $100; Maize Satin Rose Bowl, Metal Pedestal 40-2-3, $225; **Row 2:** 12" Panel Grape Crimpt Bowl, Metal Basket 55-1-1, $105; 13" Toy Rose Wedding Bowl, Metal Pedestal 103-22-3, $120; 13" Boquet Wedding Bowl, Metal Basket 101-12-1, $100.

Page From Ca. 1967 Catalog: **Row 1:** 6" Polynesian Rose Candy Box & Cover 99-52, $65; 6" Mallow Rose Candy Box & Cover 99-53, $65; 10" Vase, Crimpt Top 75-6, $50; 10" Vase, Crimpt Top 75-7, $45; 10" Vase, Crimpt Top 75-5, $125; **Row 2:** 9" Yellow Rose Crimpt Bowl 112-14, $70; 10" Paisley Apothecary Jar 99-50, $65; 8" Paisley Apothecary Jar 99-49, $55; 6" Paisley Apothecary Jar 99-48, $45; 6" Paisley Candy Box & Cover 99-51, $45; **Row 3:** 11" Yellow Rose Wedding Bowl 108-14, $75; 13" Wedding Bowl 102, $40; 13" Wedding Bowl 105, $40; **Row 4:** 13" Yellow Rose Wedding Bowl 103-14, $80; 13" Rose of Yesteryear Wedding Bowl with Foot 105-18-8, $90; 13" Wedding Bowl 102, $40.

Beaded Vase, $200, $165; Beaded Pitcher Lamp, $275; Epergne Lamp, $450; Peachblow Epergne Lamp, $450; Moss Rose Pitcher Lamp, $275; Moss Rose Crimped Top Vase, $150; Peachblow Vase, $90.

Epergne, $850; Moon & Star Oil Lamp, $125; Epergne, $850.

Row 1: Panel Grape Epergne, $110, $85; Moon & Star Covered Compote $85; Moon & Star Salver, $50; **Row 2:** Moon & Star Covered Compote, $45; Moon & Star Open Compote, $40; Satin Vase, $25; Satin Vase, $20; Epergne, $75; **Row 3:** Epergne, $65; Vase Satin, $20; Vase Satin, $30; Vase Satin, $25; Panel Grape Epergne, Vase & Bowl, $225.

All Beaded: **Row 1:** Vase, $175, $65; Jack in Pulpit Vase, $165, $200; Vase, $165; **Row 2:** Pitcher, $195, $250, $195, $85, $200; **Row 3:** Cream & Sugar (2 sets), $75 each; Peachblow, $85 each; **Row 4:** Rose Bowl, $125; Tumbler, $45, $45, $50.

Row 1: Fern Vase, $145; Vase, $75; Peachblow "Star" Vase, $95; "Star" Satin Vase, $35; "Cherry" Vase, $85; "Opal Lattice" Vase, $135. **Row 2:** "Acorn" Syrup, $95; Moss Rose Small Vase, $125; Moss Rose Medium Vase, $145; Moss Rose Large Vase, $155; "Rose" Lamp, $125; "Rose" Large Vase, $135; "Rose" Medium Vase, $105; "Rose" Small Vase, $95; Plume Miniature Lamp, $125.

All Blue Overlay Satin, Decorated: **Row 1:** Fluted Barber Bottle 1-17D, $150; Milk Pitcher 1-10D, $95; Spooner 1-14D, $55; **Row 2:** Fluted Cruet 1-15D, $75; Vine Cruet 1-7D, $75; Cream Pitcher 1-11D, $65; **Row 3:** Round Cruet 1-16D, $75; Vine Salt & Pepper 1-8D, $55 pair; Small Rose Bowl 1-6D, $65; **Row 4:** Sugar Shaker 1-9D, $95; Large Rose Bowl 1-5D, $75.

All Wild Rose Satin, Decorated: **Top:** Fairy Lamp 1-3D, $175; Candy Box 1-4D, $95; Barber Bottle 1-1D, $175; **Bottom:** Rose Bowl 1-4D, $85; Cruet 1-2D, $95.

Page from 1977 Catalog. All Overlay Decorated: **Row 1:** Oval Barber Bottle, Light Blue 1-1D, $150; Fairy Lamp 1-3D, $159; Oval Cruet, Light Blue 1-2D, $75; **Row 2:** Vine Cruet, Dark Blue 1-7D, $95; Tall Cream, Dark Blue 1-11D, $75; Sugar Shaker, Amber 1-9D, $75; Spooner, Amber 1-14D, $45; **Row 3:** Small Rose Bowl, Dark Blue 1-6D, $85; Milk Pitcher, Amber 1-10D, $65; **Row 4:** Vine Salt & Pepper, Dark Blue 1-8D, $75 pair; Large Rose Bowl, Amethyst 1-5D, $85.

The L. G. Wright Glass Company
New Martinsville, W. Va. 26155

AMETHYST OVERLAY

All Amethyst Overlay, Decorated: **Row 1:** Pickle Jar 1-12D, $85; Spooner 1-14D, $65; Fluted Cruet 1-15D, $85; Round Cruet 1-16D, $85; Fluted Barber Bottle 1-17D, $155: **Row 2:** Vine Salt & Pepper 1-8D, $65 pair; Sugar Shaker 1-9D, $105; Milk Pitcher 1-10D, $115; Tall Cream 1-11D, $75; **Row 3:** Small Rose Bowl 1-6D, $75; Vine Cruet 1-7D, $85; **Row 4:** Fairy Lamp 1-3D, $165; Oval Barber Bottle 1-1D, $150; Oval Cruet 1-2D, $85.

Satin Custard Ware, Moss Rose Decoration: **Top:** Milk Pitcher 73-4, $95; **Middle:** Lamp, 21" 930-CMR, $175; Tall Cream 73-5, $55; **Bottom:** Sugar Shaker 73-1, $95; Water Pitcher 73-3, $155; Tumbler 73-2, $35.

Custard Decorated: **Left:** Gold Floral: Water Pitcher 73-3, $135; Tumbler 73-2, $30; Large Basket 73-6, $175; Tall Cream 73-5, $45; Sugar Shaker 73-1, $85; Milk Pitcher 73-4, $75. **Right:** Strawberry: Water Pitcher 73-3, $135; Tumbler 73-2, $30; Milk Pitcher 73-4, $75; Large Basket 73-6, $175; Tall Cream 73-5, $45; Sugar Shaker 73-1, $85.

Right to left: Candy Jars & Apothecary Jars with Metal Covers & Handles: **Row 1:** Candy Boxes: Rose Floral 99-68SP, $45; Antique Golden Poppy 99-64SP, $45; Brown Apple 99-42SP, $45; Mountain Poppy 99-61SP, $45; Polynesian Rose 99-52SP, $45; **Row 2:** Apothecary Jars: Brown Apple, 6" 99-45SP, $45; Spring Bouquet, 6" 99-21SP, $45; Grey Rose, 6" 99-21SP, $45; Amber Daisy Candy Box 99-25SP, $45; **Row 3:** Apothecary Jars: Grey Rose, 8" 99-22SP, $55; Spring Bouquet, 8" 99-22SP, $55; Holland Rose, 8" 99-39SP, $55.

Woodrose Decoration: **Row 1:** Ball Vase 99-83, $25; Slim Vase 99-86, $25; **Row 2:** Apothecary Jars: 6" 99-80, $45; 8" 99-81, $55; 10" 99-82, $65; **Row 3:** Candy Box 99-88, $45.

Row 1: Holland Rose Apothecary Jars: 10" 99-40, $65; 8" 99-39, $55; 6" 99-38, $45. 6" Holland Rose Candy Jar 99-31, $45; **Row 2:** Spring Boquet Apothecary Jars: 10" 99-23, $65; 8" 99-22, $55; 6" 99-21, $45. 6" Rose Candy Jar 99-37, $55; 6" Daisy Candy Jar 99-36, $55; **Row 3:** Brown Apple Apothecary Jars: 10" 99-47, $65; 8" 99-46, $55; 6" 99-45, $45. 6" Brown Apple Candy Jar 99-42, $45; 6" Daisy Candy Jar 99-25, $45; **Row 4:** Grey Rose Apothecary Jars: 10" 99-23, $65; 8" 99-22, $55; 6" 99-21, $45. 6" Rose Candy Jar 99-26, $45; 6" Rose of Yesteryear Candy Box 99-9, $45.

Catalog Page "New Items for 1985" [All made by Gibson Glass, Milton, WV]: **Row 1:** Vine Cruet 1-7, $35 each; Fluted Cruet 1-15, $35 each; **Row 2:** Cruet 77-130, $35 each; Cream & Sugar 99-1, $20 each piece; **Row 3:** Sugar Shaker 96-2, $55 each; Oval Cruet 94-6, $35 each; Rose Bowl 98-6, $35; Basket 98-16, $45 each; **Row 4:** Vine Cruet 1-7, $55 each; Fluted Cruet 1-15, $55 each; Cruet 77-130, $55 each; **Row 5:** Tall Creamer 90-2, $30 each; Sugar Shaker 96-2, $75 each; Oval Cruet 94-6, $55 each; **Row 6:** Rose Bowl 98-6, $55; Basket 98-16, $65 each; Paperweight 77-132, $25 each; Paperweight 77-131, $20 each; Birds 77-133, $20 each.

RICH COBALT BLUE DECORATED
MARY GREGORY - (Boy or Girl)

71-2 Tumbler
71-1 Water Pitcher
71-5 Large Basket
71-3 Oval Cruet
71-4 Barber Bottle
Page 3

Rich Cobalt Blue Decorated, Mary Gregory (Boy or Girl): **Top:** Tumbler 71-2, $55; Water Pitcher 71-1, $225; **Middle:** Large Basket, $265; **Bottom:** Oval Cruet, $125; Barber Bottle 71-4, $90.

Custard Glass page from 1969 Catalog. **Row 1:** Cherry Toothpick 7-8, $22; S Toothpick 77-63, $22; S Cup 77-110, $15; Grape Tumbler 920, $18; Cosmos Tumbler 800-3, $20; Grape & Daisy Tumbler 905, $18; Wheat Tumbler 900, $18; **Row 2:** Daisy & Button Medium Slipper 22-58, $15; Daisy & Button Kitten Slipper 22-57, $18; 6" Cherry Scroll Compote 7-3, $24; 7" Hen 70-8, $40; 5" Hen 80-7, $35; 5" Owl 80-10, $35; **Row 3:** Twig Round Nappy 825-1, $12; Twig Crimpt Nappy 825-1, $15; Twig 7" Plate 825-2, $15; Beaded Shell Mug 9-12, $18; Cherry Sugar 9-5, $18; Cherry Cream 9-4, $20; **Row 4:** Tankard Pitcher 913, $20; Tankard Pitcher 914, $28; Cosmos Plate 800-2, $35; Cosmos 7" Crimpt Bowl 800-1, $28; Argonaut Bowl, 11" 911, $40; Argonaut Bowl 5" 910, $12; **Row 5:** Holly Crimpt Bowl 810-1, $35; Holly Plate 12" 810-2, $40; Peacock 11" Crimpt Bowl 820-1, $55; Peacock Plate 12" 820-2, $65; **Row 6:** Grape & Fruit Plate 805-3, $40; Grape & Fruit Crimpt Bowl 805-1, $35; Grape & Fruit 10-1/2" Round Bowl 805-2, $35.

Custard Glass. **Row 1:** Cosmos 7" Crimpt Bowl Decorated 800-1-12, $35; Grape Tumbler 6 oz. Decorated 920-15, $30; Grape & Daisy Tumbler Decorated 6 oz. 905-14, $30; Cosmos Tumbler Decorated 6 oz. 800-3-12, $38; Cosmos Plate Decorated 9" 800-2-12, $45; **Row 2:** Cosmos 7" Crimpt Bowl 800-1, $28; Grape Tumbler 6 oz. 920, $18; Grape & Daisy Tumbler 6 oz. 905, $18; Cosmos Tumbler 6 oz. 800-3, $20; Cosmos Plate 9" 800-2, $35; **Row 3:** Argonaut 11" Bowl 911, $40; Argonaut Stemmed Jelly 924, $35; Argonaut 5" Bowl 910, $12; Argonaut Tumbler 6 oz. 926, $20; **Row 4:** Argonaut Salt & Pepper 927, $42 pair; Argonaut Toothpick 925, $24; **Row 5:** Cherry Sugar 7-5, $18; Cherry Cream 7-4, $20; Wheat Tumbler 7 oz. 900, $18; S Toothpick 77-63, $22; Cherry Toothpick 7-8, $22.

Custard Ware. **Row 1:** Peacock 11" Bowl Crimpt 820-1, $55; Grape & Fruit 12" Bowl Crimpt 805-1, $35; Grape & Fruit 10-1/2" Round Bowl 805-2, $35; **Row 2:** Peacock 12" Plate 820-2, $65; Holly 12" Plate 810-2, $40; **Row 3:** Peacock 10-1/2" Round Bowl 820-3, $55; Holly 10-1/2" Round Bowl 810-3, $35; **Row 4:** 7" Hen on Nest 70-8, $40; 5" Owl 80-10, $35; Cherry 6" Compote 7-3, $24; **Row 5:** 5" Hen 80-7, $35; Daisy & Button Kitten Slipper 22-57, $18; Daisy & Button Medium Slipper 22-58, $15.

NOTE: L. G. Wright has reproduced items in this pattern since 1936. Originally this was the Palace (a.k.a. Moon & Star) pattern by Adams & Co., Pittsburgh, in the 1890s.
Row 1: Round Butter & Cover 44-2, $40; 6" Low Covered Compote, $38; 13-1/2" Plate 44-51, $45; 6" High Covered Compote 44-9, $42; 4" Covered Compote 44-8, $38; **Row 2:** Large Cream 44-16, $18; Large Sugar & Cover 44-38, $22; 8" Medium Open Compote 44-14, $30; 10" Salver 44-33, $38; Spooner 44-37, $20; **Row 3:** Salt & Pepper 44-31, $30 pair; Finger Bowl 44-21, $15; 8" Small Salver 44-34, $32; 8" Plate 44-26, $35; Crimpt Compote 44-12, $28; **Row 4:** Tumbler 44-41, $14; Champagne 44-7, $20; Goblet 44-22, $18; Juice Glass 44-25, $12; Footed Sauce Dish 44-35, $10; Salt Dip 44-30, $12.

109

Row 1: Ashtray 8" 44-1, $30, $25, $45, $35, $30, $45; **Row 2:** Spooner 44-37, $25; Large Sugar & Cover 44-38, $30; Large Cream 44-16, $25; Low Sugar & Cover 44-52, $25; Butter & Cover Round 44-2, $35; Tumbler 44-41, $35, $18, $20, $25; **Row 3:** 6" Nappy Crimpt or Flared 44-43, $25; Rose Bowl 44-44, $55; Flower Bowl with Block 44-45, $75; Low Sugar & Cover 44-52, $50, $35; Champagne 44-7, $24, $40; Cruet 44-17, $85, $65, $85; **Row 4:** Finger Bowl 44-21, $20, $16, $18; Juice Glass 44-25, $25, $18, $14, $20; Small Footed Bowl, $28, $16.

Row 1: 9" Candlestick 44-3, $35 blue each, $27 amber each; 11" Console Bowl 44-5, $65 blue, $45 amber; **Row 2:** Daisy & Button Shell Bowl 22-10, $65, $85, $85; **Row 3:** 6" Candlestick 44-4, $24 blue each, $20 amber each; 8" Console Bowl 44-6, $50 blue, $35 amber.

Row 1: Stem Covered Candy Box 6" 44-47, $65, $45, $95, $50; S Plate 8" 77-74, $22, $12; **Row 2:** Stem Open Compote Flared 7" 44-48, $65, $38, $32, $30; S Plate 8" 77-74, $15, $15; **Row 3:** Stem Covered Jelly 4-1/2" 44-50, $40, $85, $55, $45; S Sherbet 77-76, $22, $12; **Row 4:** Stem Open Compote Flared 5" 44-49, $30, $28, $55, $35; S Sherbet 77-76, $18, $18.

12" Bowl, Crimped or Flared 44-46, $45 amber either style, $65 blue either style, $50 green either style; 13-1/2" Plate 44-51, $45, $50, $65.

Row 1: Covered Compotes 44-8, $55, $48, $48, $38, $80; **Row 2:** High Footed Covered Jellies 44-50, $45, $85, $40; Large Sugar & Cover 44-38, $65, $45, $30; **Row 3:** High Footed Compotes 44-9, $40, $65, $85, $55, $55; **Row 4:** Low Footed Compotes 44-10, $55, $48, $38, $80; **Row 5:** Large Covered Compotes 44-11, $65, $125, $70, $85, $85.

Row 1: Open Compotes 44-12, $38, $48, $30, $65; **Row 2:** Medium Open Compotes 44-14, $35, $45, $70, $55; **Row 3:** Water Pitchers 44-56, $225, $195, $150, $125; **Row 4:** Large Open Compotes 44-15, $48, $55, $70, $95; **Row 5:** Salvers 44-32, $50, $90; Large Open Compote 44-15, $55; **Row 6:** Salvers 44-32, $50, $50, $45.

Row 1: Wines 44-42, $35, $15, $15, $20; Decanters 44-18, $75, $95, $175 ruby with crystal stopper only; **Row 2:** Low Sugars & Cover 44-52, $35, $50, $25; Large Creams 44-16, $35, $50, $25; **Row 3:** Salts & Peppers 44-31, $22, $38, $18, $28; Sugar Shakers 44-54, $105, 65, $85, $55; Rectangular Relishes 44-29, $35, $25; **Row 4:** Nappies Crimpt 44-43, $35, $18, $30, $24; Juice Glasses 44-25, $14, $16, $20, $25; **Row 5:** Tumblers 44-41, $25, $20, $35, $18; Ice Teas 44-23, $25, $20, $32, $40; Spooners 44-37, $35, $50, $25; **Row 6:** Round Butters & Covers 44-2, $45, $55, $85; Console Set 44-4-6, $75 set; **Row 7:** Handled Relishes 44-27, $25, $22, $32; Oval Relishes 44-28, $15, $25, $18.

Catalog Page from 1959. All Cherry. **Row 1:** Crimpt 3 Footed Bowl, $18, $20, $24; Tumbler 7-9, $15; Water Pitcher 7-10, $35, $45; **Row 2:** 2 Handled Footed Bowl, $26, $20, $20; 6" Crimpt Bowl 7-3, $18; **Row 3:** 2 Handled Footed Crimpt Bowl, $20, $18, $22; Salver 7-7, $32; **Row 4:** 4 Footed Crimpt Bowl, $30, $24; Crimpt Compote, $35; Scalloped Bowl, $20; **Row 5:** Small Crimpt Bowl, $12, $18; Cream 7-4, $15, $22, $30.

All Cabbage Leaf. **Row 1:** Wine 77-70, $20; Sherbet, $18; Goblet 77-19, $25; Covered Candy Dish, $85, $60; Goblet 77-19, $20; Sherbet, $15; Wine 77-70, $18; **Row 2:** Wine 77-70, $20; Sherbet, $15; Goblet 77-19, $25; Covered Candy Dish, $65, $95; Goblet 77-19, $30; Sherbet, $20; Wine 77-70, $25; **Row 3:** Open Compote, $30, $35; Footed Bowl, $35; Salver, $40; Open Compote, $25 each; **Row 4:** Footed Mint, $35, $30, $25, $25; Flared Sherbet, $15, $20, $25, $15.

Row 1: Daisy & Button Fan Vase, $25; Moon & Star Vase, $40; Beaded Large Ivy Bowl 3-5, $58; Moon & Star Vase, $30; Daisy & Button Fan Vase, $35; **Row 2:** All Beaded: Large Crimpt Bowl 3-3, $35; Large Flared Bowl 3-3, $48; Large Ivy Bowl 3-5, $38; Large Flared Bowl 3-3, $42; Large Crimpt Bowl 3-3, $48; **Row 3:** All Beaded: Large Crimpt Bowl 3-3, $40; Large Ivy Bowl 3-5, $50; Large Flared Bowl 303, $38; Large Ivy Bowl 3-5, $42; Large Crimpt Bowl 3-3, $42; **Row 4:** All Beaded: Large Crimpt Bowl 3-3, $38; Large Ivy Bowl 3-5, $45; Large Flared Bowl 3-3, $35.

Row 1: High Footed Covered Jelly 4-1/2" 44-50, $40; Cream 44-18, $75; Spooner 44-37, $35; Large Sugar & Cover 44-38, $95; Water Pitcher 1 qt. 44-56, $125; **Row 2:** Covered Jelly 3-1/2" 44-24, $50; Wine 2 oz. 44-42, $45; Juice 5 oz. 44-25, $20; Goblet 9 oz. 44-22, $30; Sherbet 44-36, $12; **Row 3:** Ice Tea 11 oz. 44-23, $25; Tumbler 7 oz. 44-11, $35; Low Sugar & Cover 44-52, $25; Salt & Pepper 44-31, $45 pair; Sugar Shaker 44-54, $105; **Row 4:** Ash Tray 8-1/2" 44-1, $45; Ash Tray 5" 44-53, $20; Toothpick 44-39, $18; Salt Dip 44-30, $18; Soap Dish 44-55, $45.

Row 1: Moon & Star 10" Salver 44-33, $50; Moon & Star Goblet 44-22, $20; Moon & Star 8" Compote 44-14, $45; Sawtooth Goblet 77-35, $20; Panel Daisy Goblet 77-31, $20; Moon & Star 6" Covered Compote 44-9, $55; **Row 2:** Daisy & Button 6" Covered Compote 22-20, $48; Daisy & Button 4" Round Covered Compote 22-17, $38; Daisy & Button Oval Covered Butter 22-12, $40; Daisy & Button Thumbprint Panel Goblet 22-30, $25; Daisy & Button Thumbprint Panel Wine 22-69, $18; Daisy & Button Thumbprint Panel Sugar 22-24, $24; Daisy & Button Thumbprint Panel Cream 22-23, $24; **Row 3:** Daisy & Button 6-1/2" Handled Nappy 22-35, $25; Daisy & Button 8" Scalloped Plate 22-41, $25; Daisy & Button 10" Round Plate 22-39, $35; Moon & Star Wine 44-42, $20; Daisy & Button Square Footed Sherbet 22-52, $24.

Row 1: Daisy & Button 10" Plate 22-39, $40, $30; Daisy & Button Thumbprint Panel Water Pitcher 22-37, $85, $65; Daisy & Button Cream 22-21, $28, $22, $22; **Row 2:** Daisy & Button Pickle Jar 22-36, $55, $75; Daisy & Button Bell Candy Box 22-70, $40, $50, $65; Daisy & Button Large Fan Tray 22-65, $30, $45; **Row 3:** Daisy & Button 4" Round Covered Compote 22-17, $48, $30, $38, $35, $40; Daisy & Button 9 oz. Tumbler 22-67, $15, $18; Daisy & Button Crimpt Rose Bowl 22-44, $30, $45, $35, $38; **Row 4:** Daisy & Button Thumbprint Panel Sugar 22-24, $20, $28; Daisy & Button Thumbprint Panel Cream 22-23, $20, $28; Daisy & Button Thumbprint Panel Sherbet 22-52, $20, $28; Daisy & Button Flower Bowl with Block 22-58, $45; Daisy & Button Oval Butter & Cover 22-12, $48, $35.

All Daisy & Button. **Row 1:** 7" Round Plate 22-40, $15; Tall Covered Sugar 22-22, $20; Tall Cream 22-21, $19; Fan Tray 22-65, $45; 10" Round Plate 22-39, $40; Square Plate, $35; 6" Square Ash Tray 22-3, $15; **Row 2:** 5" Oval Bowl, 4 toed 22-8, $20; Finger Bowl 22-27, $18; Cruet 22-25, $55; 6" Square Ash Tray 22-3, $25; 11-1/2" Canoe 22-16, $50; Pickle Jar & Cover 22-36, $65; Spooner or Vase 22-60, $55; Gypsy Kettle & Cover 22-31, $28, $22; **Row 3:** Small Fan Ash Tray 22-2, $15; Boot Match Holder, $28; 6" Crimpt Bowl 22-5, $15; Tumbler 22-67, $15; Daisy & Button Thumbprint Panel Wine 22-69, $18; Daisy & Button Thumbprint Panel Goblet 22-30, $20; Goblet 22-29, $18; Wine, $15; Rose Bowl 22-44, $35; 4" Square Sauce 22-50, $12; **Row 4:** Bar Glass, $18; Ash Tray, $10; Salt Dip, $15; Small Slipper 22-59, $24; Baby Bootie, $16; Medium Slipper 22-58, $12; Kitten Slipper 22-57, $22; Salt & Pepper 22-47, $45 pair; Large Hat, $45; Medium Hat 22-32, $16; Rolled Edge Hat, $22; Small Hat 22-33, $18.

All Daisy & Button—Small Sleighs also came with candleholder center. **Row 1:** Canoe 22-16, $30, $50, $65; **Row 2:** Covered Compote 4" 22-17, $40, $48, $35, $38, $30, $38; Pickle Jar 22-36, $90, $75, $55; **Row 3:** 10" Oval 4 Footed Bowl 22-7, $75, $45; Small Shell Footed Bowl 22-72, $60, $38, $50; **Row 4:** 10" Oval 4 Footed Bowl 22-7, $48, $55, $48, $38; **Row 5:** 11" Star Berry Bowl 22-11, $38, $45, $75, $55; **Row 6:** Sleigh, Large 22-56, $160, $60; Sleigh, Small 22-54, $95, $40; **Row 7:** Sleigh, Large 22-56, $120, $110; Sleigh, Small 22-54, $55, $45.

Row 1: Moon & Star 9" Candlestick 44-3, $45 each; Moon & Star 11" Console Bowl 44-5, $85; Daisy & Button Shell Footed Bowl 22-10, $115; **Row 2:** Moon & Star 8-1/2" Ash Tray 44-1, $45; Moon & Star 6" Candlesticks 44-4, $35 each; Moon & Star Low Console Bowl 44-6, $65; **Row 3:** Daisy & Button Toothpick 22-63, $20; Bird Salt Dip 77-56, $18; Daisy & Button Oval Butter & Cover 22-12, $55; Daisy & Button Thumbprint Panel Sugar 22-4, $35; Daisy & Button Thumbprint Panel Cream 22-23, $35.

All Double Wedding Ring. **Row 1:** 6" Covered Compote 11-1, $24, $28, $35, $20, $28; **Row 2:** 4" Jelly Compote & Cover 11-2, $28, $35, $20, $28, $24; Toothpick 11-6, $17, $16, $20, $15, $12; **Row 3:** Wine 11-7, $15, $12, $20, $17, $16; 8" Plate 11-4, $18, $15; Sherbet 11-5, $18, $15; **Row 4:** 8" Plate 11-4, $14, $12, $10; Sherbet 11-5, $14, $12, $10.

All Eye Winker. Row 1: Marmalade & Cover 25-25, $25, $18, $20, $22; 4" Covered Compote 25-14, $35, $30, $25, $27; **Row 2:** Pickle Tray 25-21, $20, $18; Covered Butter 25-12, $40, $35, $55; **Row 3:** Honey Dish & Cover 25-20, $30, $50, $35; 6" Vase 25-28, $35, $30, $28, $25; **Row 4:** Low Footed Open Compote 25-17, $25, $20, $18; Low Footed Covered Compote 25-15, $40, $35, $55; **Row 5:** High Footed Open Compote 25-2, $30, $35, $40, $25; Water Pitcher 25-26, $75, $55; **Row 6:** High Footed Covered Compote 25-1, $75, $55, $45, $60; Water Pitcher 25-26, $65, $95.

Row 1: All Eye Winker: Tumbler 25-27, $18, $15, $20, $16; Marmalade & Cover 25-25, $22, $25, $20, $18; **Row 2:** All Eye Winker: 6" Vase 25-28, $25, $35, $28, $30; Water Pitcher 25-26, $65, $55, $75, $95; **Row 3:** Grape 10" Oval Bowl 77-90, $65, $80, $55, $50, $45; **Row 4:** All Wildrose: 7" Ash Tray 77-86, $9, $7, $10, $12, $8; 6" Ash Tray 77-87, $8, $6, $9, $10, $7; 4" Ash Tray 77-88, $7, $5, $8, $9, $6.

Page from 1967 Catalog. **Row 1:** All Eye Winker: 5" 4 Toed Bowl 25-11, $12 each; 10" Footed bowl 25-10, $55, $30, $35; **Row 2:** All Eye Winker: Sherbet 25-4, $18, $16, $12, $4; Salt or Pepper Shaker 25-24, $20, $24, $15; Round Sauce 25-5, $15, $12, $12, $18; **Row 3:** All Eye Winker: Covered Sugar 25-19, $20, $25, $18; Cream 25-18, $18, $20, $15; Tumbler 25-27, $16, $20, $18, $15; **Row 4:** All Panel Grape: Sherbet 55-18, $12, $22, $18, $15; Sugar & Cream 55-5 (3 sets), $28 set, $35 set, $30 set; **Row 5:** All Panel Grape: Covered Jelly 55-8, $45, $35, $40, $30; 8" Plate 55-12, $30; 10" Plate 55-11, $45; Sugar & Cream 55-5, $48; Demitasse Cup & Saucer 55-6, 55-17, $45 set; **Row 6:** All Panel Grape: Covered Compote 55-3, $65, $85, $45, $50; Water Pitcher 55-9, $125; **Row 7:** All Panel Grape: 12" Crimpt Bowl 55-1, $75; 15" Plate 55-10, $75; Punch Set 55-14, $325; Lily Bowl-Torte Plate 55-2, $75.

PANEL GRAPE PATTERN

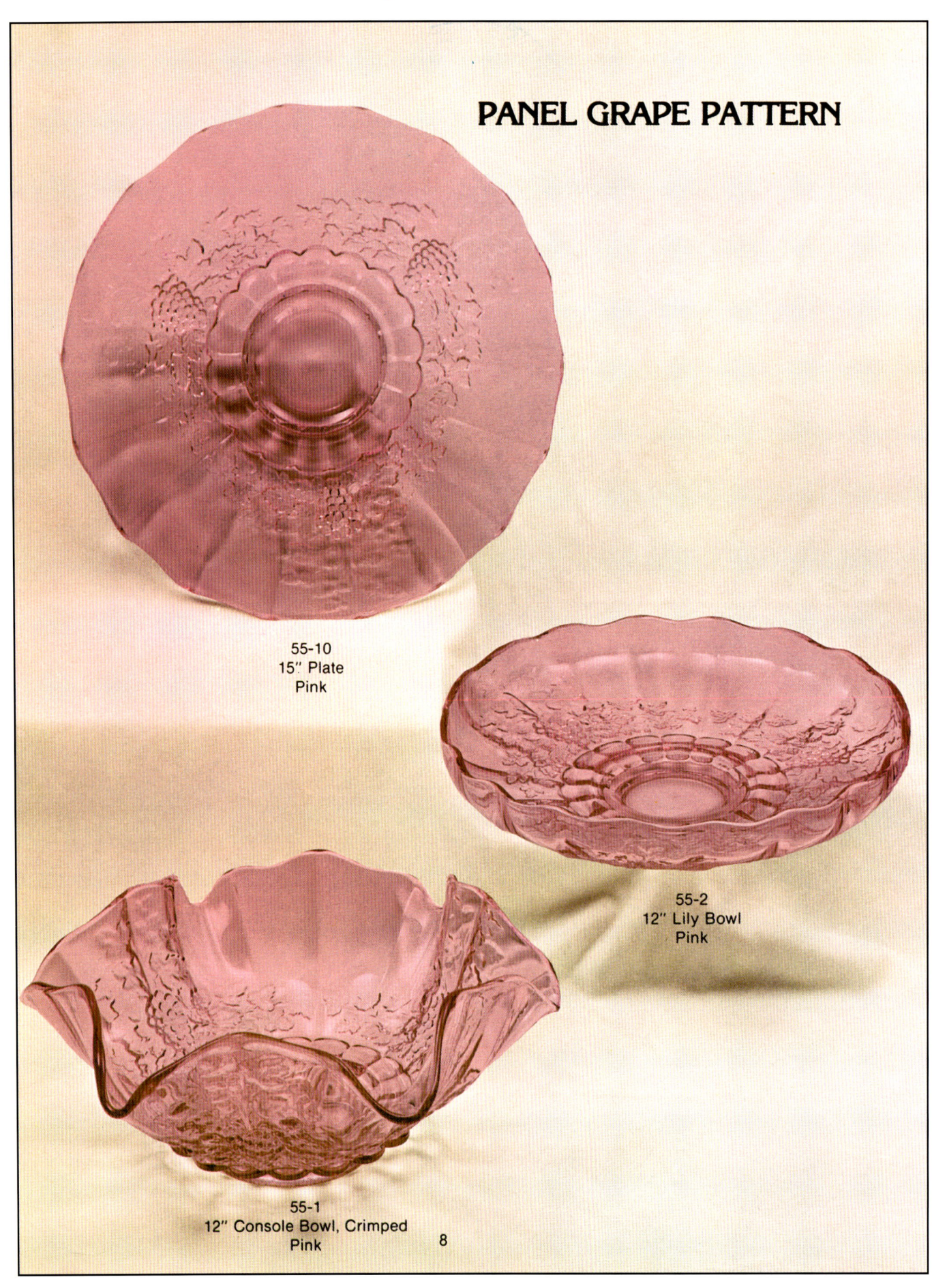

55-10
15" Plate
Pink

55-2
12" Lily Bowl
Pink

55-1
12" Console Bowl, Crimped
Pink

All Panel Grape in Pink. **Row 1:** 15" Plate 55-10, $48; **Row 2:** 12" Lily Bowl 55-2, $55; **Row 3:** 12" Crimped Console Bowl 55-1, $55.

All Panel Grape—prices given for crystal. **Row 1:** Large Creamer, $18; Large Covered Sugar, $22; Water Pitcher 55-9, $35; 10" Plate 55-11, $25; Large Celery Vase, $45; 6" Celery Vase, $35; **Row 2:** Covered Jelly 55-8, $25; Cup 55-6 & Saucer 55-17, $25 set; 8" Plate 55-12, $18; Small Sugar 55-5, $12; Small Cream 55-5, $12; **Row 3:** 8" Nappy, $20; Goblet 55-7, $15; Footed Ice Tea or Parfait, $15; 14 oz. Ice Tea, $12; 5" Nappy, $10; 4" Nappy, $8; **Row 4:** Tumbler 55-19, $10; Old Fashion, $10; Cocktail, $12; Tall Sherbet 55-18, $12; Wine 55-20, $12; Cordial, $15.

Milk Glass. **Row 1:** Panel Grape Water Pitcher 55-9, $45; Moon & Star Lamp, $175; Beaded Lamp, $125; Daisy & Cube Lamp, $95; Plume Lamp, $125; Beaded Grape Covered Compote, $38; **Row 2:** Beaded Grape Goblet 5-3, $18; Panel Grape Goblet 55-7, $18; Panel Grape Ice Tea, $20; Panel Grape Sherbet 55-18, $14; Panel Grape Wine 55-20, $16; Panel Grape Cream & Sugar, $24 set; Panel Grape 4" Covered Jelly 55-8, $35; **Row 3:** Panel Grape 10" Plate 55-11, $55; Panel Grape 8" Bowl, $48; Panel Grape 8" Plate 55-12, $24; Panel Grape Small Bowl, $18.

All Panel Grape in Ruby. **Row 1:** 4" Round Nappy 55-16, $20; Small Sugar & Cream 55-5, $48 set; Goblet 55-7, $35; 4" Covered Jelly 55-8, $45; Sherbet 55-18, $22; Wine, $55-20, $25; **Row 2:** Demitasse Cup & Saucer 55-6-17, $45 set; 10" Plate 55-11, $45; 15" Plate 55-10, $75; 8" Plate 55-12, $30; Water Pitcher 55-9, $125; **Row 3:** Lily Bowl-Torte Plate 55-2, $75; 15 Piece Punch Bowl Set 55-14, $325; 12" Crimpt Bowl 55-1, $75.

All Ruby. **Row 1:** Horn of Plenty Goblet 77-26, $30; Panel Grape Goblet 55-7, $35; Panel Grape Water Pitcher 55-9, $125; Moon & Star Decanter 44-18, $175; Daisy & Cube Goblet 77-21, $30; Moon & Star Goblet 44-22, $45; Herringbone Goblet 77-25, $30; **Row 2:** Hobnail Goblet 33-8, $30; Daisy & Button Thumbprint Panel Goblet 22-30, $30; Jersey Swirl Goblet 35-5, $30; Strawberry & Currant Goblet 77-36, $30; Stipple Star Goblet 59-6, $30; Diamond Quilted Goblet 77-23, $30; Sweetheart Goblet 77-37, $30; **Row 3:** S Toothpick 77-63, $24; Hobnail Salt & Pepper Shakers 33-10, $45 pair; Panel Grape Wine 55-20, $25; Diamond Quilted Wine 77-66, $25; Daisy & Button Thumbprint Panel Wine 22-69, $25; Moon & Star Wine 44-42, $35; Moon & Star Salt & Pepper Shakers 44-31, $76 pair; Moon & Star Toothpick 44-39, $35; Moon & Star Salt Dip 44-30, $25; Daisy & Button Round Salt Dip 22-45, $18; Daisy & Button Triangular Salt Dip 22-46, $20.

Row 1: Magnet & Grape Jelly Compote 4" 37-3, $26, $30, $35, $24, $26; **Row 2:** Magnet & Grape Goblet 37-2, $24, $20, $20, $30, $15; **Row 3:** Magnet & Grape Champagne 37-1, $18, $18, $20, $15, $22; Magnet & Grape Wine 37-5, $15, $18, $18, $25, $20; **Row 4:** Large Rabbit Candy Box 70-10, $20; Magnet & Grape Sherbet 37-4, $20, $16, $12, $14, $14; **Row 5:** 5" Cat Candy Box 80-2, $25, $20, $50; 5" Dog Candy Box 80-4, $50, $25.

Maple Leaf Pattern

Row 1: All Maple Leaf: Compote 42-4, $20; Water Pitcher 42-6, $35; Butter & Cover 42-3, $35; **Row 2:** All Maple Leaf: 10" Salver 42-9, $28; Toothpick 42-8, $15; Sugar & Cover 42-2, $20; Cream 42-1, $18; **Row 3:** Hibiscus Satin Candy Box 99-D-11SSP, $45; Maple Leaf Tumbler 42-5, $16; Maple Leaf Spooner 42-7, $18.

All Priscilla. **Row 1:** 7" Ash Tray 56-5, $14, $18, $10, $12, $10; **Row 2:** 8" Plate 56-7, $18, $14, $12, $12; 6-1/2" Nappy Crimpt 56-6, $15; **Row 3:** Rose Bowl 56-8, $30, $35, $45, $30, $25; 6-1/2" Nappy Crimpt 56-6, $12, $14, $10; **Row 4:** Wine 56-10, $20, $25, $12, $12, $14; Sherbet 56-9, $10, $8, $12, $18, $16.

Row 1: S Goblet 77-34, $18, $15, $30, $22, $18; **Row 2:** S Wine 77-71, $12, $14, $25, $18, $14; Priscilla 4" Covered Jelly 56-1, $25, $45; **Row 3:** Priscilla Goblet 56-2, $15, $15, $18, $30; Priscilla 4" Covered Jelly 56-1, $30 each; **Row 4:** Priscilla Round Sauce 56-3, $12, $10, $10; Priscilla Toothpick 56-4, $16, $25, $18, $16, $14.

STORCK and RUSHES
CRYSTAL SATIN

All Stork & Rushes. **Row 1:** Tumbler 78-6, $12; Water Pitcher 78-1, $38; **Row 2:** Covered Sugar 78-4, $15; Cream 78-5, $15; Spooner 78-3, $15; **Row 3:** Sauce 78-7, $8; Berry Bowl 78-2, $20.

All Stork & Rushes. **Row 1:** Tumbler 78-6, $16; Water Pitcher 78-1, $50; **Row 2:** Covered Sugar 78-4, $25; Cream 78-5, $20; Spooner 78-3, $20; **Row 3:** Sauce 78-7, $10; Berry Bowl 78-2, $30.

All Thistle, All Crystal. **Row 1:** 6" Covered Compote 64-18, $20; 6" Flared Compote 64-17, $12; Spoon 64-16, $12; Water Pitcher 64-19, $28; **Row 2:** Tall Sugar 64-23, $12; Tall Cream 64-22, $12; Cruet 64-20, $22; Sugar 64-9, $10; Cream 64-8, $10; **Row 3:** 7-1/2" Bowl 64-2, $15; Honey Dish 64-10, $22; 5" Bowl 64-1, $8; Sauce 64-21, $5; **Row 4:** Goblet 64-3, $15; Wine 64-7, $12; Tumbler 64-24, $10; Sugar Shaker 64-15, $24; Salt & Pepper 64-14, $18 pair; Toothpick 64-12, $10; Salt Dip 64-6, $7; **Row 5:** 8" Oval Relish 64-5, $8; 7-1/2" Square Plate 64-4, $10; Covered Butter 64-11, $28.

All Three Face, All Crystal with Satin Stems. **Row 1:** Spooner 65-15, $22; Cream 65-11, $24; Covered Sugar 65-12, $28; **Row 2:** 4" Covered Compote 65-2, $30; 6" Covered Compote 65-1, $35; **Row 3:** Salt Dip 65-6, $12; Toothpick 65-9, $12; Goblet 65-3, $18; **Row 4:** Salt & Pepper 65-7, $28 pair; Sugar Shaker 65-14, $35; Wine 65-10, $15; Sherbet 65-8, $15.

All Westward Ho, All Satin Crystal. **Row 1:** 5" Low Round Covered Compote 66-6, $35; 6" Oval Covered Compote 66-1, $45; **Row 2:** 6" Round Covered Compote 66-2, $40; Covered Butter 66-8, $45; Covered Sugar 66-10, $30; **Row 3:** Celery Vase 66-11, $25; Cream 66-9, $24; 4" Covered Compote 66-7, $30; **Row 4:** Sherbet 66-4, $15; Tumbler 66-12, $15; Wine 66-5, $15; Goblet 66-3, $18.

All Crystal or Crystal Satin. **Row 1:** Cabbage Leaf Goblet 77-19, $20; Lion Goblet 77-28, $20; Thistle Goblet 77-38, $15; Priscilla Goblet 56-2, $15; Priscilla Jelly Compote & Cover 56-1, $25; Daisy & Button Thumbprint Panel Goblet 22-30, $18; Panel Grape Goblet 55-7, $15; Sawtooth Goblet 77-35, $15; Jersey Swirl Goblet 35-5, $15; **Row 2:** All Three Face: Sherbet 65-8, $15; 4" Compote & Cover 65-2, $30; 6" Compote & Cover 65-1, $35; Goblet 65-3, $18; Wine 65-10, $15; Toothpick 65-9, $12; Salt Dip 65-6, $12; Salt & Pepper 65-7, $28 pair; **Row 3:** Westward Ho: Sherbet 66-4, $15; Wine 66-5, $15; Goblet 66-3, $18; 6" Compote & Cover 66-6, $35; Tall Compote & Cover 66-2, $40; Oval Compote & Cover 66-1, $35; Lion Bread Plate 77-49, $25; **Row 4:** All Moon & Star: Salt Shaker 44-31, $15; Spooner 44-37, $20; Wine 44-42, $15; Goblet 44-22, $18; Water Pitcher 44-56, $65; Covered Sugar 44-38, $22; Cream 44-16, $18; Handled Jelly Dish 44-27, $18; **Row 5:** All Eye Winker: Covered Sugar 25-18, $18; Cream 25-19, $15; Salt Shaker 25-24, $15; Covered Compote 25-1, $45; Goblet 25-3, $15; Covered Butter 25-12, $35.

Page from 1967 Catalog. **Row 1:** Wildrose Individual Butter & Cover 77-101, $24, $20; Tree of Life 3 Toed Sauce 60-6, $8, $8, $12; **Row 2:** All Tree of Life: Finger Bowl 60-3, $8, $12; Crimpt Nappy 60-5, $8, $12, $8; **Row 3:** All Tree of Life: Finger Bowl 60-3, $8; Deep Crimpt Bowl 60-1, $10, $10, $15; **Row 4:** Handled Relish 60-7, $18; Footed Crimpt Compote 60-9, $22; Wine 60-8, $12, $12, $16; **Row 5:** Goblet 60-4, $20, $15, $15; Covered Tall Compote 60-2, $35, $25, $30; **Row 6:** All Eye Winker: 8" Vases 25-30, $35, $25, $28, $30.

Row 1: All Wildflower: Sugar & Cover 67-4, $24; Cream 67-3, $18; Stick Candy Jar & Cover 67-10, $38, $30; Sugar & Cover 67-4, $20; Cream 67-3, $15; **Row 2:** Wildflower Footed Sauce Dish 67-9, $10, $8; Wildflower Covered Compote 67-2, $24, $20; Wildrose Compote 72-6, $16, $12, $16; **Row 3:** Wildrose Tall Compote 72-7, $18, $25, $16, $20; Wildrose Compote 72-6, $16, $20; **Row 4:** Embossed Rose 6" Covered Candy Box 70-3, $27, $27, $25, $35; Embossed Rose 4" Covered Candy Box 70-15, $20, $24, $22; **Row 5:** Wildrose 9" Nappy, 3 toed 77-78, $24, $22, $20, $22; **Row 6:** Wildrose Covered Compote 70-16, $28, $30, $25, $35; Wildrose 12 oz. Ice Tea 77-73, $12, $12, $18, $15.

Row 1: Thousand Eye Goblet 77-43, $20, $15, $15; Diamond Quilted Goblet 77-23, $20, $18, $18, $15, $30; Thistle Goblet 65-3, $15, $15, $18, $20; **Row 2:** Moon & Star Goblet 44-22, $22, $45, $18, $26, $30; Panel Grape Goblet 55-7, $18, $15, $20, $25, $35, $18; **Row 3:** Rose Sprig Goblet 77-105, $20, $15, $15; Beaded Grape Goblet 5-3, $15, $18, $18; Wildflower Goblet 67-5, $15, $15, $20; Thumbprint Goblet, $15, $18, $15; **Row 4:** Two Panel Goblet 77-39, $15, $15; Diamond Panel Fruit Goblet, $20, $15; Sweetheart Goblet 77-37, $15, $15, $30, $22; Maple Leaf Goblet 77-29, $20, $30, $25, $25; **Row 5:** Acorn Goblet 77-17, $15, $15, $20; King's Crown Goblet, $15, $18; Plume Goblet 77-32, $15, $17; Daisy & Cube Goblet 77-21, $20, $20, $25.

Row 1: Goblets: Hobnail 33-8, $15, $15, $18, $15; Cabbage Leaf 77-19, $30, $20, $25; Herringbone 77-25, $15, $30, $15, $15, $20; **Row 2:** Goblets: Artichoke 77-18, $20; Paneled Daisy 77-31, $15; New England Pineapple, $15; Daisy & Cube 77-21, $15, $15, $30, $18, $20, $18; Horn of Plenty 77-26, $15; Cabbage Rose 77-19, $15; Unidentified, $15; **Row 3:** Goblets: Broken Column 77-102, $15; One O One 77-42, $15; Three Face 65-3, $18; Lion 77-28, $20; Strawberry & Currant 77-36, $22, $18, $15, $30, $15, $18; Deer & Pine Tree 77-103, $18; Shell & Tassel 77-106, $18; Frosted Ribbon 77-104, $18; **Row 4:** Goblets: Daisy & Button 22-24, $18, $15, $24; Jersey Swirl 35-5, $15, $15, $20; Daisy & Button Thumbprint Panel 22-30, $20, $15, $30, $20, $25, $17; **Row 5:** Wines: Daisy & Button Thumbprint Panel 22-69, $22, $15, $18; Wildflower 67-12, $18, $15, $12; Daisy & Button, $15, $20; Cabbage Leaf 77-70, $15, $25, $18, $20; Panel Grape 55-20, $12, $25; Westward Ho 66-5, $15.

Row 1: Goblets: Thousand Eye 77-43, $15, $20; Daisy & Button 22-29, $18, $24; Inverted Dot 77-27, $15; Horn of Plenty 77-26, $30; Maple Leaf 77-29, $25; **Row 2:** Wines: Daisy & Button Thumbprint Panel 22-69, $27, $18, $22, $27, $15, $18; Magnet & Grape 77-84, $20, $18, $25, $15, $18; **Row 3:** Panel Grape Goblet 55-7, $35, $18, $20, $25, $20; Wildflower Wine 67-12, $25, $15, $18; Cabbage Leaf Wine Satin 77-70, $25, $15; **Row 4:** Goblets: Daisy & Button Thumbprint Panel 22-30, $30, $25, $30, $20, $17, $20; Herringbone 77-25, $30, $15, $15.

Row 1: Goblets: Plume 77-32, $15; Shell & Tassel 77-106, $18; Frosted Ribbon 77-104, $19; Morning Glory 77-30, $15; Lion 77-28, $20. Lion Bread Plate, $25; **Row 2:** Goblets: Acorn 77-17, $15; Maple Leaf 77-29, $15; Artichoke 77-18, $29; Deer & Pine Tree 77-103, $18; Rose Sprig 77-105, $15; Broken Column 77-102, $15; **Row 3:** Cabbage Leaf Goblet 77-19, $25; Cabbage Leaf Wine 77-70, $25; Grasshopper Goblet 77-24, $20; Diamond Quilted Goblet 77-23, $30; Diamond Quilted Wine 77-66, $12; Daisy & Cube Goblet with Forest Etch 77-22, $35; **Row 4:** Daisy & Cube Goblet with Flower Band Décor 77-21-10, $18; Daisy & Cube Wine with Flower Band Décor 77-81-10, $30; Daisy & Cube Goblet 77-21, $30; Daisy & Cube Wine 77-81, $12; Strawberry & Currant Goblet 77-36, $45; Strawberry & Currant 77-68 Wine, $18.

Row 1: Wild Rose Goblet, $30; Wild Rose Sherbet, $18; Wild Rose Wine, $24; Stipple Star Goblet 59-6, $22, $15, $17, $15, $17; **Row 2:** Morning Glory Goblet 77-30, $15; Morning Glory Wine, $12; Thistle Wine 64-7, $15, $12, $12; Moon & Star Cruet 44-16, $65; Grasshopper Goblet 77-24, $20, $15, $25, $20; **Row 3:** Melon Handled Bon Bon, $22, $28; Thistle Sherbet, $12, $15, $12; Melon Handled Bon Bon, $22, $18; **Row 4:** Crescent Planter 77-48, $28, $20, $22, $22.

Row 1: Thumbprint: Tumbler 97-1, $15, $10, $15; Water Pitcher 84-1, $95, $65, $95; **Row 2:** Maple Leaf Vase, $18, $20; Beaded Grape Square Covered Compote 5-1, $28, $24; Daisy & Button Cream, $22; Thumbprint Sugar Shaker 96-1, $95; **Row 3:** Thumbprint Tall Cream 90-1, $25, $20; Diamond Quilted Goblet 77-23, $18, $15; Hobnail Goblet 33-8, $15, $15, $18; Thumbprint Round Cruet 95-1, $50, $30; **Row 4:** Daisy & Button Salt Shaker 22-47, $18, $22, $18; Beaded Grape Salt Shaker, $12, $15, $18; Fluted Vine Salt Shaker 77-55, $15, $12, $15, $15; Beaded Grape 4" Square Nappy 5-5, $12, $9.

Row 1: Maple Leaf Compote 72-4, $30, $40, $25, $25; **Row 2:** Moon & Star 3-1/2" Covered Jelly 44-24, $35, $48; Diamond Quilted Wine 77-66, $12, $14, $18, $25, $12; Cabbage Leaf Wine 77-70, $25; Panel Grape Wine 55-20, $12, $18, $12; **Row 3:** Stipple Star Wine 59-7, $18, $12; Sweetheart Wine 77-82, $12, $25; Daisy & Cube Wine 77-81, $12 each; Eye Winker Wine 25-7, $18, $12, $25, $12; **Row 4:** Dolphin Compote 72-3, $55; Sweetheart Covered Sugar & Cream 77-11 (3 sets), $25, $48, $40; **Row 5:** Moon & Star Sherbet 44-36, $20, $12; Moon & Star Soap Dish 44-55, $45, $30, $25, $20; **Row 6:** Hobnail Compote 33-3, $16, $22, $12; Daisy & Cube Compote 72-1, $15, $15, $25.

Row 1: Daisy & Button 4 Toed Candleholder 22-14, $25 each; Daisy & Button 10" 4 Toed Bowl 22-7, $48; Beaded Crimpt Candleholder 3-1, $20 each; Beaded Crimpt Footed Bowl 3-3, $35; **Row 2:** Daisy & Button 4 Toed Candleholder 22-14, $30 each; Daisy & Button Star Bowl 22-11, $95; Beaded Crimpt Candleholder 3-1, $22; Beaded Crimpt Bowl 3-3, $38; Daisy & Button Large Shell Footed Bowl 22-10, $75.

Row 1: Daisy & Button Punch Set 22-43, $275; **Row 2:** Panel Grape Punch Set 55-14, $350; Daisy & Button Punch Set 22-42, $250.

Row 1: Panel Grape 6" Covered Compote 55-3, $50; Daisy & Button Thumbprint Panel Stick Candy Jar 22-61, $75, $55, $85, $55, $55; Panel Grape 6" Covered Compote 55-3, $45; **Row 2:** All Panel Grape: 8" Open Compote 55-4, $25, $22, $32; 6" Covered Compote 55-3, $85, $65, $50; **Row 3:** All Panel Grape: 9" Salver 55-15, $24, $35; 8" Open Compote 55-4, $45; 9" Salver 55-15, $27, $48; **Row 4:** Violin Candy Box 70-14, $55, $48; Panel Grape 9" Salver 55-15, $27; Violin Candy Box 70-14, $68, $55.

Row 1: Strawberry & Currant Open Compote 72-5, $20, $25, $15, $17; S Cruet 77-12, $25, $35, $45, $28; **Row 2:** All Cherry: Sugar 7-5, $28, $12; Cream 7-4, $32, $15; Water Pitcher 7-14, $95, $40, $55; **Row 3:** All Cherry: Sugar 7-5, $20, $28, $14; Cream 7-4, $22, $30, $16; Tumbler 7-9, $15, $12; **Row 4:** Pump & Trough Set 77-95-96, $30, $35; Cherry Butter & Cover 7-2, $30, $35, $45; **Row 5:** Stove Candy Box 70-11, $55, $38, $55, $65; Flat Iron Candy Box 70-5, $35, $60; **Row 6:** 12" Oval 4 Toed Grape Bowl 70-90, $65, $55; Flat Iron Candy Box 70-5, $50 each; **Row 7:** 12" Oval 4 Toed Grape Bowl 70-90, $55, $80; Violin Candy Box 70-14, $50, $68, $48.

Row 1: Cherry Water Pitcher 7-14, $40, $95, $55; Moon & Star Water Pitcher 44-56, $125, $195, $150, $65, $225; **Row 2:** Wildrose Goblet 77-41, $20; Wildrose Compote 72-6, $20, $15; Wildrose Goblet 77-41, $30; Wildrose Compote 72-6, $30; Wildrose Goblet 77-41, $15; Wildrose Compote 72-6, $15; **Row 3:** Ribbed Palm Leaf Wine, $15, $25, $15; Wildrose Goblet 77-41, $15; Cherry Wine, $25, $15, $18, $15; **Row 4:** All Priscilla: Low Covered Candy, $35, $20, $28, $24, $24; Small Round Nappy, $20, $15, $12, $12; **Row 5:** Moon & Star Soap Dish 44-55, $35, $45, $20, $25; Double Wedding Ring Small Footed Tumbler (4) $12, $12, $20, $15.

Row 1: Wildrose Goblet 77-41, $17, $30; Wildrose Compote 72-6, $15; Wildrose Goblet 77-41, $20, $15, $15; **Row 2:** Wildrose Wine 77-69, $12, $15, $18, $25, $12; Wildrose Compote 72-6, $30, $17; **Row 3:** Princess Feather Goblet 77-33, $15; Princess Feather Tulip Sundae 77-57, $15; Princess Feather Goblet 77-33, $20; Princess Feather Tulip Sundae 77-57, $20; Princess Feather Goblet 77-33, $15; Princess Feather Tulip Sundae 77-57, $15; **Row 4:** Embossed Rose 6" Candy Box 70-3, $24, $22, $20; Wheat & Barley Goblet 77-40, $22, $15.

Row 1: Corn Vase 77-121, $95, $35, $65; Jersey Swirl Covered Compote, High Footed 35-2, $28, $25, $45, $38; Petticoat Vase, $15, $15, $18; **Row 2:** Jersey Swirl 4" Covered Compote 35-1, $20, $40, $32, $22; Dolphin Footed Compote 72-3, $25, $38, $28; **Row 3:** Beaded Grape Cruet 5-2, $45, $65, $55; Beaded Grape Footed Covered Compote 5-1, $24; Beaded Grape 8" Square Plate 5-4, $15; Beaded Grape Goblet 5-3, $18, $30, $15; **Row 4:** Jersey Swirl Goblet 35-5, $15; Jersey Swirl Crimpt Compote 35-4, $15, $30, $15, $22.

Row 1: Thistle: 7-1/2" Square Plate 64-4, $12, $15, $10, $12; Goblet 64-3, $15, $20, $15, $18; **Row 2:** Moon & Star Covered Compote 44-8, $48, $38, $80, $38, $55, $38; **Row 3:** Daisy & Button 6" Square Ash Tray 22-3, $18, $15, $10, $15; Hobnail Tumbler 33-11, $15, $10, $12, $12; **Row 4:** S Cruet 77-12, $65, $55, $48, $45; 7" Hen on Nest 70-8, $40; Pressed Honeycomb Rose Bowl, $45, $28; Pressed Honeycomb Rose Bowl Ruffled, $55; **Row 5:** Hobnail Sugar Shaker, $17, $10, $12; Three Face Salt & Pepper Shakers 65-7, $28 pair; Three Face 4" Covered Compote 65-2, $30; "Rustic" Vase, 4 Footed, $18, $22; Swan Salt Dip 77-52, $15, $15, $18, $12.

Row 1: Acorn & Squirrel Candy Box, $35, $45, $55; Daisy & Button Thumbprint Panel Covered Compote 22-19, $75, $75, $125; **Row 2:** Jersey Swirl Crimpt Compote 35-4, $15, $22; Jersey Swirl Goblet 35-5, $20, $15; Daisy & Button 6" Oval 4 Toed Covered Compote 22-18, $28, $38, $30; **Row 3:** Sweetheart Goblet, $30; One O One Goblet 77-42, $15; Horn of Plenty Goblet 77-26, $15; Sweetheart Cream 77-41, $30; Sweetheart Covered Sugar 77-41, $30, $18; Inverted Dot Goblet 77-27, $15; Diamond Panel Fruits Goblet, $15, $20; **Row 4:** Strawberry & Currant Goblet 77-36, $18; Daisy & Cube Goblet 77-21, $18; Moon & Star Salt Shaker 44-31, $15; Daisy & Button Gypsy Kettle & Cover 22-31, $22, $22, $28; S Toothpick 77-63, $12, $18, $12; Daisy & Button Salt Dip 22-45, $10; Daisy & Button 9 oz. Tumbler 22-67, $15; Hobnail Finger Bowl 33-7, $18.

Row 1: Moon & Star Covered Sugar 44-38, $70; Moon & Star 4" Covered Compote 44-8, $85; Priscilla 4" Covered Compote 56-1, $45; Cherry Cream 7-4, $32; Cherry Sugar 7-5, $30; Wildrose Open Compote 72-6, $32; Eye Winker 4" Covered Compote 25-14, $38; Eye Winker 6" Vase 25-28, $38; **Row 2:** Cherry Butter & Cover 7-2, $35; Mirror & Rose Goblet 77-79, $18; Moon & Star 4" Covered Compote 44-8, $50; Daisy & Button 4" Covered Compote 22-17, $35; Daisy & Button Basket 22-4, $28; Jersey Swirl Goblet 35-5, $15; Trough & Pump 77-96-95, $38; **Row 3:** Moon & Star Goblet 44-22, $35; Hobnail Goblet 33-8, $20; Moon & Star 4" Covered Compote 44-8, $58; 7" Hen on Nest 70-8, $45; Embossed Rose 4" Covered Candy Box 70-15, $28; Daisy & Button Rose Bowl 22-44, $48; Moon & Star 6" Covered Compote 44-9, $60; **Row 4:** Beaded Small Footed Compote 3-2, $18; Strawberry & Currant Goblet 77-36, $15; Hobnail Covered Bowl 33-2, $18; Wildrose 8" 3 toed Nappy 77-78, $25; Daisy & Button 5" Oval Bowl, 4 Toed 22-8, $15; Daisy & Button Rose Bowl 22-44, $32; Daisy & Button 4" Covered Compote 22-17, $30; Daisy & Button Thumbprint Panel Goblet 22-30, $15; **Row 5:** Daisy & Button 5" Oval Bowl, 4 toed 22-8, $20; Wildrose Goblet 77-41, $18; Wildrose Covered Compote 70-16, $30; Moon & Star Butter & Cover 44-2, $50; Moon & Star Low Covered Sugar 44-52, $35; Moon & Star Cream 44-16, $30; Moon & Star Goblet 44-22, $30.

Row 1: 7" Hen on Nest 70-8, $60, $55; Daisy & Button Thumbprint Panel Covered Compote, $175; Daisy & Button 10" Plate 22-39, $50; Daisy & Button 7" Square Plate, $38; **Row 2:** Moon & Star Goblet 44-22, $65; Wildflower Goblet 67-5, $45; Daisy & Button Thumbprint Panel Goblet 22-30, $60; Wildflower Covered Compote 67-1, $85; Strawberry & Currant Goblet 77-36, $45; Jersey Swirl Goblet 35-5, $45; Daisy & Button Square Ash Tray 22-3, $28; **Row 3:** Moon & Star Wine 44-42, $45; Wildflower Wine 67-12, $45; Daisy & Button Thumbprint Panel Wine 22-69, $40; Cherry Sugar 7-5, $35; Cherry Cream 7-4, $45; Daisy & Button Thumbprint Panel Square Sugar 22-4, $30; Daisy & Button Thumbprint Panel Square Cream 22-23, $35.

Row 1: Baltimore Pear Goblet 77-112, $15; Baltimore Pear Plate, $15; 9-1/2" Wildflower Square Plate 67-6, $18; Wildflower Covered Compote, $25; Wildflower Goblet 67-8, $15; Wildflower Wine 67-12, $12; **Row 2:** Thistle Round Plate, $10; 7-1/2" Thistle Square Plate 64-4, $10; Thistle Large Round Plate, $15; Thistle 7-1/2" Bowl 64-2, $15; Thistle Goblet 64-3, $15; **Row 3:** Beaded Grape Salt & Pepper, $24 pair; Beaded Grape Goblet 5-3, $15; Beaded Grape 8" Square Plate 5-4, $15; Beaded Grape Covered Compote 5-1, $20; Beaded Grape 4" Square Nappy 5-5, $8; Thistle Salt Dip 64-6, $7; **Row 4:** Thousand Eye Goblet 77-43, $15; Thousand Eye Square Plate, $12; Rose In Snow Round Bread Plate, $25; Lord's Supper Bread Plate, $25.

All Crystal. **Row 1:** Cabbage Leaf Wine 77-70, $18; Paneled Sawtooth Wine 77-77, $12; Paneled Sawtooth Sherbet 77-80, $12; Cherry Covered Butter Dish 7-2, $28; Moon & Star 8" Low Compote & Cover 44-10, $38; Moon & Star Round Butter & Cover 44-2, $40; **Row 2:** All Eye Winker: Tumbler 25-27, $12; Wine 25-7, $12; Large Open Compote 25-2, $20; Water Pitcher 25-26, $45; Honey Dish & Cover 25-20, $25; **Row 3:** All Westward Ho: Cream 66-9, $24; Covered Butter 66-8, $45; Covered Sugar 66-10, $30; 4" Covered Compote 66-7, $30; Celery Vase 66-11, $25; **Row 4:** All Thistle: 7-1/2" Square Plate 64-4, $10; 7-1/2 Bowl 64-2, $15; 5-1/2" Bowl 65-1, $8; 8" Oval Relish 64-5, $8; Goblet 64-3, $15; Wine 64-7, $12; Salt Dip 64-6, $7; **Row 5:** All Goblets: Maple Leaf 77-29, $20; Artichoke 77-8, $15; Frosted Ribbon 77-104, $18; Plume 77-32, $8; Acorn 77-17, $15; Deer & Pine Tree 77-103, $18; Rose Sprig 77-105, $15; Shell & Tassel 77-106, $18; Broken Column 77-102, $15.

Milk Glass; **Row 1:** Daisy & Button Crimpt Compote, $45; Daisy & Button 13" Salver 22-48, $55; Daisy & Button 10" Oval Bowl, 4 toed 22-7, $38. **Row 2:** Moon & Star 6" Covered Compote 44-9, $55; Moon & Star 4" Covered Compote 44-8, $38; Moon & Star 10" Salver 44-33, $45; Daisy & Button 5" Oval Bowl, 4 toed 22-8, $12; Moon & Star 8" Open Compote 44-18, $38. **Row 3:** "Open Edge" Plate, $15; Daisy & Button Canoe 22-16, $30; Daisy & Button Pickle Jar 22-36, $55; Open Lattice Edge Plate, $19.

All Milk Glass. **Row 1:** Moon & Star 8" Open Compote 44-18, $38; Moon & Star 6" Covered Compote 44-9, $55; Daisy & Button "Banana Boat", $55; **Row 2:** Acorn Covered Candy Box, $18; Moon & Star 10" Salver 44-33, $45; Stipple Star Goblet 59-6, $18; Embossed Rose Rose Bowl 75-4, $20; **Row 3:** Daisy & Button Sandal, $12; Colonial Carriage Ash Tray 77-1, $15; Frog Toothpick 77-60, $15; Chick Basket Toothpick 77-129, $15; Daisy & Button Anvil, $15; Daisy & Button Cart Ash Tray 22-1, $15.

All Milk Glass. **Row 1:** Strawberry & Currant Goblet 77-36, $18; Strawberry & Currant Compote 72-5, $18; Hobnail Sugar Shaker, $35; Fluted Vine Salt & Pepper 77-55, $35 pair; Daisy & Button Spooner 22-60, $38; S Cruet 77-12, $45; **Row 2:** Vase, $24; Maple Leaf Vase, $24; Cherry Sugar 7-5, $15; Cherry Cream 7-4, $17; Daisy & Cube Compote, $20; Daisy & Cube Goblet 77-21, $18; **Row 3:** S/Inverted Strawberry Compote, $20; Flat Iron Candy Box 70-5, $45; Daisy & Button Kitten Slipper 22-57, $15; Daisy & Button Medium Slipper 22-58, $12; Daisy & Button Small Slipper 22-59, $10; Swan Salt Dip 77-52, $14; Dolphin Compote 72-3, $39.

Row 1: Mirror & Rose Pickle Jar 77-108C, $150; Daisy & Button Pickle Jar 22-36, $130; Mirror & Rose Spooner, $95; Daisy & Button Spooner 22-60, $85; Daisy & Button Rose Bowl 22-44, $75; Wildrose 6" Crimpt Compote 72-6, $55; Queen Anne Slipper 77-92, $30; Strawberry & Currant Crimpt Compote 72-5, $55; **Row 2:** Strawberry & Currant Wine 77-68, $35; Double Wedding Ring Wine 11-7, $35; Strawberry & Currant Goblet 77-36, $45; Wildrose Goblet 77-41, $45; Double Wedding Ring Goblet 11-2, $45; Cherry Toothpick 7-8, $30; Daisy & Button Candy Jar 22-17, $65; Embossed Rose Fairy Lamp 34, $175; **Row 3:** Three Face Salt & Pepper 67-5 (2 pair), $45 pair, $35 pair; All Argonaut: Tumbler 926, $45; Toothpick 925, $35; Salt & Pepper 927, $65 pair; Footed Compote 924, $48; **Row 4:** All Argonaut: Covered Butter 921, $125; Cream 922, $55; 5" Bowl 910, $40; 11" Bowl 911, $95; **Row 5:** All Argonaut: Toothpick 925, $24; Salt & Pepper 927, $42 pair; Tumbler 926, $20; Covered Sugar 923, $40; Footed Compote 924, $24; Covered Butter 921, $50.

Page from 1977 Supplement Catalog. **Row 1:** Dahlia Tumbler 2-2, $25; Dahlia Water Pitcher 2-1, $85, $45; **Row 2:** Cherry Ice Tea 7-15, $20, $30; Panel Grape Large Cream 55-22, $35; Panel Grape Large Sugar 55-21, $48; **Row 3:** All Purple Slag: Cherry Sugar 7-5, $22; Cherry Cream 7-4, $22; Cherry Butter 7-2, $38; Trough 77-96, $15; Pump 77-95, $30; **Row 4:** All Cherry Purple Slag: Goblet 7-12, $20; Ice Tea 7-15, $18; Tumbler 7-9, $18; Water Pitcher 7-14, $45.

171

Row 1: Yellow Rose Lamp 750, $115; Thistle Large Goblet 64-38, $15; Dahlia Goblet 2-3, $15; Thistle 10" Plate 64-37, $15; Daisy & Button Lamp 591, $95; Wildflower Stick Candy 67-10, $20; Embossed Rose Lamp 74-C, $125. **Row 2:** All Cherry Red Slag: Toothpick 7-8, $25; Sugar 7-5, $25; Cream 7-4, $25; Tumbler 7-9, $22; Water Pitcher 7-14, $45.

Row 1: Thumbprint Syrup 69A-1, $150; Daisy & Button Bell 22-73, $30; Bicentennial Bell 1776, $18; **Row 2:** Thumbprint Ice Tea Tumbler 97A-1, $25; Fern Ice Tea Tumbler 97A-2, $45; Daisy & Button Wine 22-69, $20; Daisy & Button Goblet 22-30, $25; Daisy & Button Water Pitcher 22-37, $95; **Row 3:** Stars & Stripes Tumbler 97-8, $65; Wildrose Wine 77-69, $28; Wildrose Goblet 77-41, $35; **Row 4:** Herringbone Goblet 77-25, $30; Hobnail Bowl, $18; Hobnail Rose Bowl, $38; Hobnail Finger Bowl Underplate, $12; Hobnail Fingerbowl & Underplate, $40; **Row 5:** All King's Crown with Forest Etch: Cordial, $25; Wine, $25; Goblet, $30; Sherbet, $22; Fingerbowl, $24.

Page from 1967 Supplement Catalog. **Row 1:** Lamp Shades Decorated Golden Rambling Rose 99-60-GRR, $45, Sunset Rose 99-60-SR, $45, Mountain Poppy 99-60-MP, $45; Mirror & Rose Pickle Caster in Frame 77-108-5, $165; Mirror & Rose Pickle Jar 77-108, $45, $50, $85; **Row 2:** Mirror & Rose Salt Shaker 77-1-7, $15, $18, $24; Butterfly Ash Tray 77-109, $12, $18, $12; Daisy & Cube Goblet, Flower Band Décor 77-21-10, $18, $35, $18; Daisy & Cube Wine, Flower Band Décor 77-81-10, $30, $15; **Row 3:** 9" Cosmos Plate, Pansy Decoration 800-2-12, $45; Grape Tumbler, Decorated 920-5, $18; Grape & Daisy Tumbler, Decorated 905-14, $18; Cosmos Crimpt Bowl, Pansy Decoration 800-1-12, $35; Cosmos Tumbler, Decorated 800-3-12, $20 each; **Row 4:** Moss Rose Tankard Pitcher 913-40, $95; Moss Rose Vine Tankard Pitcher 914-40, $135; Rose Vine Tankard Pitcher 913-17, $75; Rose Vine Tankard Pitcher 914-17, $120; Peachblow Round Cruet, Moss Rose 95-40, $95; Peachblow Cream, Moss Rose 90-40, $85; **Row 5:** Cherry Scroll 6" Open Compote, $20; 5" Owl on Nest Candy Box 80-10, $45; 5" Hen on Nest Candy Box 80-7, $50; 5" Rooster on Nest Candy Box 80-12, $50; Daisy & Button Kitten Slipper 22-57, $22; Daisy & Button Medium Slipper 22-58, $18; Daisy & Button Small Slipper 22-59, $15; S Toothpick 77-63, $22; Cherry Toothpick 7-8, $22; **Row 6:** Cherry Ruffled Sugar 7-5, $25; Cherry Cream 7-4, $25; Atterbury Duck Candy Box 70-2, $125; 7" Hen on Nest Candy Box 70-8, $80; 5" Duck on Nest Candy Box 80-5, $50; 5" Swan on Nest Candy Box 80-14, $45.

Row 1: Dolphin Compote 72-3, $55; Cherry Cream 7-4, $32; Hobnail Rose Bowl 33-7, $40; 7" Hen on Nest 70-8, $45; Hobnail Finger Bowl 33-7, $28; Daisy & Button Thumbprint Panel Wine 22-69, $30; Daisy & Button Thumbprint Panel Goblet 22-30, $40; **Row 2:** Cherry Basket, $75; Beaded Grape Goblet 5-3, $18; Beaded Grape 8" Plate 5-4, $15; Beaded Grape Goblet 5-3, $15; Beaded Grape 8" Plate 5-4, $18; Beaded Grape Goblet 5-3, $18; Thistle Plate 64-4, $10; Cherry Cream 7-4, $38; Panel Grape Water Pitcher 55-9, $95; **Row 3:** Herringbone Goblet 77-25 (5), $20, $15, $30, $15, $15; Large Turtle Covered Dish, $60; 7" Hen on Nest 70-8, $55; Maple Leaf Goblet 77-29 (2), $20, $35; Daisy & Cube Goblet 77-21 (3), $15, $18, $24; **Row 4:** Two Panel Goblet 77-39, $15; Beaded Compote, $28; Daisy & Button Small Hat 22-33, $20; Daisy & Button Medium Hat 22-32, $16; Daisy & Button Small Hat 22-33, $12; Daisy & Button Medium Hat 22-32, $28; Paperweight (4), $45 each; Moon & Star Salt Dip 44-30, $12; Daisy & Button Bar Glass, $24; Moon & Star Salt Dip 44-30, $20; Daisy & Button Bar Glass, $14; Stars & Stripes Tumbler 97-8, $65; Stars & Stripes Tall Cream 90-8, $145; Shell & Tassel Vase, $125.

Page from ca. 1959 Catalog. **Row 1:** Daisy & Button Large 4 Wheel Cart, $95, $40; Daisy & Button Medium 4 Wheel Cart, $35, $35; **Row 2:** Daisy & Button Medium 4 Wheel Cart, $45; Fish Covered Dish 70-4, $48, $48, $35; Daisy & Button Medium 4 Wheel Cart, $35; **Row 3:** Small One Handled Basket, $15, $15, $18, $15; Large One Handled Basket, $20, $20; Beaded Small Ivy Bowl 3-4, $35; Large One Handled Basket, $20, $28; Vase, $15, $15, $18.

Page from ca. 1959-1960 Catalog. **Row 1:** Daisy & Button Large 4 Wheel Cart, $95, $60, $55, $40; **Row 2:** Daisy & Button Medium 4 Wheel Cart, $35, $35; Daisy & Button Large 4 Wheel Cart, $45; Daisy & Button Medium 4 Wheel Cart, $35, $45; **Row 3:** Three Wheel Cart 77-9, $60, $45, $65, $100; **Row 4:** Moon & Star 13" Oval Boat Shaped Relish 44-40, $35, $30, $25; **Row 5:** Moon & Star Toothpick 44-39, $18, $35, $25, $15, $20, $18, $18; Daisy & Button Medium 4 Wheel Cart, $35; Diamond Quilted Wine 77-66, $12, $14, $12, $18, $25.

Row 1: Acorn Covered Candy Box, $22, $18, $18, $27, $18, $15, $20; **Row 2:** Daisy & Button 4" Round Covered Compote 22-17, $35, $40, $30, $38; Daisy & Button Mustard with Wire Handle, $28; Embossed Rose Salt Shaker 77-54, $15, $27, $18, $22; **Row 3:** Frog Toothpick 77-60, $18, $15, $20, $18, $28; Chick Basket Toothpick 77-129, $15, $28, $20, $20, $15, $15; **Row 4:** Daisy & Button Small 4 Wheel Cart 22-1, $18, $15, $28; Daisy & Button Anvil Ash Tray, $15, $18, $18, $26, $15; Colonial Carriage Ash Tray 77-1, $15, $15, $20, $15; **Row 5:** Leaf Ash Tray 77-3, $9, $6, $5, $6; Colonial Carriage Ash Tray 77-1, $15; Daisy & Button Small 4 Wheel Cart 22-1, $18; Daisy & Button Sandal, $15, $20, $16, $16, $15.

Row 1: Moon & Star Divided Rectangular Relish, $25; Cabbage Leaf Miniature Lamp, $85; Moon & Star Divided Rectangular Relish, $20; Cabbage Leaf Miniature Lamp, $75; Moon & Star Divided Rectangular Relish, $25; **Row 2:** Maple Leaf Compote 72-4, $27, $25, $40, $25, $30; **Row 3:** Flat Iron Covered Candy Box 70-5, $50, $65, $35, $55, $35; **Row 4:** Daisy & Button Wire Handled Ash Tray, $15, $14, $15, $18; Daisy & Button 6-1/2" Handled Nappy 22-35, $16, $18, $24, $18.

All Daisy & Button: **Row 1:** 11" Star Shaped Bowl 22-11, $45, $55, $38, $45; **Row 2:** Cheese Plate & Cover 22-74, $40, $55; 11" Star Shaped Bowl 22-11, $75; Handled Basket 22-4, $25, $22, $25, $32; **Row 3:** Miniature Stove Candleholder 22-15, $28, $22, $20, $22; 5" Star Sauce 22-51, $30, $22, $22, $25, $20; **Row 4:** Boat Ash Tray, $12, $18, $14, $12; Boat Shaped Wall Planter, $32, $22, $25, $25; Triangular Salt Dip 22-46, $12, $14, $16, $14.

Row 1: Chick Covered Basket 77-7, $25; Moon & Star 8" Ash Tray 44-1, $25, $30, $35; Shell & Tassel Covered Compote, $45; **Row 2:** Daisy & Button Thumbprint Panel Cup & Saucer, $40, $30; Daisy & Button Oval Butter & Cover 22-12, $35, $48; Daisy & Button Thumbprint Panel Sherbet 22-52, $29, $28; **Row 3:** Daisy & Button Small Round Bowl, $12, $15; Daisy & Button Thumbprint Panel Sugar & Cream 22-23, 22-24, $40, $56; Fish Ash Tray 77-2, $14, $18; **Row 4:** Bird Salt Dip 77-50, $10, $15, $12, $12; Daisy & Button Toothpick 22-63, $10, $12, $16, $12; Miniature Dust Pan 77-15, $15, $18; Three Face Toothpick 65-9, $12; Three Face Salt Dip 65-6, $12.

Row 1: 14" Slim Vase Holland Rose Decoration, $25; 14" Slim Vase, Rose of Yesteryear Decoration, $25; Wildrose Tall Covered Compote 70-16 (3), $25, $28, $35; Apothecary Jar, Holland Rose Decoration 99-40, $65; Apothecary Jar, Holland Rose Decoration 99-39, $55; Apothecary Jar, Holland Rose Decoration 99-38, $45; **Row 2:** Thumbprint Pickle Caster 98-1-5, $185; Maize Pickle Jar, $120, $95; Fern Pickle Caster 98-2-5, $275; Maize Pickle Jar, $150; Daisy & Button Pickle Jar 22-36, $85; Opal Swirl Pickle Caster 98-4-5, $225; Daisy & Button Pickle Jar 22-36 (2), $75, $55; Opal Dot Pickle Caster 98-3-5, $245; **Row 3:** Embossed Rose 4" Covered Candy Box 4 toed 70-15, $24, $22, $20; Strawberry & Currant Cream 77-94, $24, $24; Trough 77-96, $12; Pump 77-95, $23; Trough 77-96, $10; Pump 77-95, $20; **Row 4:** Queen Ann Slipper 77-92, $10, $12, $12, $15; Turkey Toothpick 77-93, $18, $16, $20, $18; Eye Winker 5-1/2" Fairy Lamp 25-29, $65, $45, $45, $90; Hi Button Shoe 77-91, $15, $15, $18, $12.

Row 1: 3" Hen 70-7, $24, $30, $26, $22; Bee Hive Honey Dish 77-8, $35, $22, $30, $26, $26; **Row 2:** Daisy & Button Toothpick Triangle 22-64, $16, $14, $22, $18, $16, $24; Daisy & Cube Sugar & Cream 77-10 (3 Sets), $30, $38, $32; **Row 3:** Sweetheart Toothpick 77-64, $24, $18, $18, $15; Rabbit Toothpick 77-61, $25, $25, $30, $20, $28; Fish Toothpick 77-59, $22, $20, $15, $18; **Row 4:** Rooster Toothpick 77-62, $20, $18, $18, $15; Cherry Salt Dip 7-6, $10, $15, $15, $10, $10; Frog Salt Dip 77-51, $15 each; **Row 5:** Fish Spoon or Ash Tray 77-2, $16, $16, $14, $18; Violin Ash Tray 77-6, $22, $15, $15, $15, $18.

Page from circa 1963 Catalog. **Row 1:** Daisy & Button 8" Scalloped Plate 22-41, $20, $15, $22, $25; Panel Sawtooth Wine 77-77, $12, $14, $18, $14; **Row 2:** Embossed Rose Triangle Nappy 77-47, $12, $12, $15; Daisy & Button Skillet 22-53, $22, $30, $24, $28; **Row 3:** Stove Covered Candy Dish 70-11, $55, $65, $38; Embossed Rose Triangle Fairy Lamp, $130, $105, $80; **Row 4:** Horseshoe Relish, $24, $24, $20; Horseshoe Covered Candy Dish 70-9, $48, $40, $48.

Page from circa 1960 Catalog. **Row 1:** Moon & Star Toothpick 44-39, $25, $20, $18, $35, $18, $25; Daisy & Button Toothpick 22-63, $12, $10, $15, $16, $20, $12; **Row 2:** Moon & Star Salt Dip 44-30, $25, $20; Daisy & Button Triangle Salt Dip 22-42, $16, $20, $14, $14, $12, $14; Daisy & Button Round Salt Dip 22-45, $15, $10, $16, $15, $18; **Row 3:** Moon & Star Salt Dip 44-30, $15, $12, $15, $12; Double Wedding Ring Toothpick 11-6, $17, $16, $15, $12, $20; Double Wedding Ring Salt Dip 11-8, $14, $10, $18, $12, $12; **Row 4:** Cherry Toothpick 7-8, $15, $14, $18, $16, $12, $18, $12; Jersey Swirl Salt Dip 35-8, $10, $12, $15, $10, $17; **Row 5:** Cherry Salt Dip 7-6, $10, $10, $15, $17, $10; Stipple Star Salt Dip 59-5, $12, $16, $14, $14, $18; **Row 6:** Eye Winker Salt Dip 25-22, $12, $16, $12; Eye Winker Toothpick 25-23, $12, $16, $12; S Toothpick 77-63, $18, $14, $24, $12; **Row 7:** Daisy & Button Triangle Toothpick 22-64, $18, $16, $16, $22, $14, $24; Sawtooth Toothpick 77-100, $15, $12, $17; **Row 8:** Priscilla Toothpick 56-4, $16, $14, $25, $18; Sweetheart Toothpick 77-64, $18, $20, $18, $18, $24, $15.

Row 1: Turkey Toothpick 77-93, $24, $18; Colonial Carriage Ash Tray 77-1, $18, $15, $15, $20, $15; **Row 2:** Turkey Toothpick 77-93, $20, $18, $15; Bird Salt Dip 77-50, $15, $12, $10, $12, $18; **Row 3:** Swan Salt Dip 77-52, $15, $15; Daisy & Button Medium Slipper 22-58, $16, $14, $18, $22, $12, $16; **Row 4:** Swan Salt Dip 77-52, $15, $18, $12; Queen Ann Slipper 77-92, $12, $15, $12, $10, $18; **Row 5:** Leaf Ash Tray 77-3, $6, $5; Hi Button Shoe 77-91, $24, $12, $15, $15, $18; **Row 6:** Leaf Ash Tray 77-3, $9, $6; Daisy & Button Slipper 22-59, $18, $15, $12, $24, $12, $15; **Row 7:** Thistle Salt Dip 77-53, $18, $14, $12; Violin Ash Tray 77-6, $18, $15, $15, $15, $22; **Row 8:** Thistle Salt Dip 77-53, $14, $15, $12; Wildflower Rectangular Salt Dip 67-7, $22, $18, $15, $15, $12.

1983 New Items

Row 1: Daisy & Button Skillet 22-53, $20, $24; Daisy & Button Cheese Plate & Cover 22-74, $35; Flat Iron Covered Candy Dish 70-5, $85, $50, $40; **Row 2:** Hen on Nest 70-8, $65; Stove Covered Candy Dish 70-11, $55, $90; Large Turtle Covered Dish 70-12, $85; **Row 3:** Violin Covered Candy Dish 70-14, $50; Three Wheel Cart 77-9, $120, $50; Rabbit Toothpick 77-61, $25; 5" Rabbit 80-11, $65; **Row 4:** Hoot Owl Relish 77-75 (3), $45, $35, $25; 5" Rabbit 80-11, $45; **Row 5:** All Argonaut: Small Nappy 910, $35; Butter 921, $125; Cream 922, $50; Sugar 923, $75; Jelly Compote 924, $45; Toothpick 925, $45; Salt & Pepper 927, $75; **Row 6:** Water Pitcher 71-1, $150; Tumbler 71-2, $35; Cruet 71-3, $85; Barber Bottle 71-4, $145; Basket 71-5, $195; Syrup 75-1, $110.

Row 1: Moon & Star 10" Lamp, $250, $225, $175, $275, $175; **Row 2:** Eye Winker 5-1/2" Fairy Lamp 25-29B, $65, 25-29R, $65; Peachblow Fairy Lamp 57-21, $165; Moss Rose Miniature Lamp 795, $145, 796, $145; Eye Winker 5-1/2" Fairy Lamp 25-29G, $45, 25-29A, $45; **Row 3:** Plume 8-1/2" Lamp 57-AO, $140, 57-PO, $165; Peachblow Fairy Lamp 57-20, $165; Plume Lamp 57-BO, $165, 57-RO, $225; **Row 4:** Beaded 10" Lamp 79-BO, $165, 79-AO, $140, 79-RO, $225, 79-PO, $165, 79-CO, $125.

All Fairy Lamps. **Row 1:** Embossed Rose 34, $165, $85, $150, $75, $95, $150; **Row 2:** Hobnail 33, $85, $140, $80, $55; **Row 3:** Moon & Star 44, $65, $165, $115; **Row 4:** Eye Winker 25-29, $95, $65, $45, $45.

Top: Thousand Eye Fairy Lamps 46, $45, $45, $40, $85, $55, $85; **Bottom:** Moon & Star Relish 44-40, $20; Thistle Handled Sauce 64-26, $14; Stork Goblet 77-114, $18; Thistle Low Covered Bowl 64-25, $24.

Page from 1976 Supplement Catalog. **Row 1:** Sweetheart Fairy Lamp 59-8G, $85, 59-8A, $75, 59-8R, $150, 59-8B, $95; **Row 2:** Stipple Star Fairy Lamp 77-115R, $150, 77-115G, $75, 77-115B, $95, 77-115A, $75.

Index

A

Acorn, 147, 150, 166
Acorn candy box, 168
Amber Overlay, 85, 86, 87, 90, 97, 98, 182, 188
Amberina, 37, 39, 51, 54, 57, 110, 122, 124, 125, 128, 155, 157, 161, 175, 180, 182, 183, 184, 185, 186
Amethyst Overlay, 97
Anvil ashtray, 168, 178
Apothecary jar, 47, 48, 90, 101, 102, 103, 182
Argonaut (Argonaut Shell), 106, 107, 170, 187
Artichoke, 148, 150, 166

B

Baby Bootie, 123
Baltimore Pear, 165
Banded Grape, 74
Barber bottle, 38, 45, 50, 52, 54, 57, 59, 62, 64, 65, 95, 96, 97, 98, 105, 187
Basket, 63, 100, 104, 105, 163, 175, 176, 180, 187
Beaded, 57, 59, 80, 82, 83, 91, 93, 118, 132, 154, 163, 175, 176, 188
Beaded Grape, 132, 147, 152, 160, 165, 175
Beaded Shell, 106
Beehive honey dish, 35, 183
Bicentennial Bell, 173
Bird figurine, 104
Bird salt dip, 125, 181, 186
Biscuit jar, 55
Blue Overlay, 58, 85, 87, 88, 89, 90, 91, 93, 95, 188
Boat ashtray, 180
Boot match holder, 123
Brides basket, 58
Broken Column, 148, 150, 166
Butterfly ashtray, 174
Butterscotch Overlay, 88, 89

C

Cabbage Leaf, 119, 144, 148, 149, 150, 153, 166, 179
Cabbage Rose, 148
Candleholder, 57, 111, 116, 125
Canoe, 123, 124, 167, 180
Carnival glass, 40, 42, 66, 67, 68, 69, 70, 71, 72, 73, 74, 75, 76, 77, 78, 79, 80, 171
Cart ashtray, 168
Celery vase, 143, 166
Cherry, 35, 41, 57, 61, 74, 106, 107, 108, 120, 157, 158, 163, 164, 166, 169, 170, 171, 172, 174, 175, 183, 185
Cherry Scroll, 35, 106, 174
Chick Basket toothpick, 178
Chick Covered Basket, 181
Christmas Snowflake, 55, 56, 63, 65
Chocolate glass, 187
Colonial Carriage ashtray, 168, 178, 186
Corn Vase, 59, 61, 160
Cosmos, 106, 107, 174
Covered Animals:
    Acorn & Squirrel, 38, 162
    Atterbury Duck, 35, 38, 41, 42, 174
    Bird, 36, 37, 39
    Cat, 40, 41, 42, 135
    Cow, 36, 37, 40, 41, 42
    Dog, 135
    Duck, 37, 39, 174
    Fish, 176
    Frog, 36, 37
    Frog covered candy, 42
    Hen, 35, 36, 37, 38, 39, 40, 41, 42, 57, 61, 74, 75, 76, 77, 106, 108, 161, 163, 164, 174, 175, 183, 187
    Horse, 36, 37, 40, 41, 42
    Lamb, 36, 37, 40, 41
    Large Rabbit, 42, 135, 187
    Large Turkey, 40
    Large Turtle, 38, 175, 187
    Owl, 36, 37, 39, 40, 41, 42, 106, 108, 174
    Rabbit, 36, 37
    Rooster, 36, 37, 39, 40, 41, 42, 174
    Swan, 36, 37, 39, 40, 41, 174
    Turkey, 37, 39, 40, 41, 42
    Turtle, 36, 37, 40, 41
Cranberry, 43, 44, 45, 46, 47, 48, 49, 50, 51, 52, 53, 54, 55, 56, 58, 81, 83, 84, 85, 93, 94, 173, 175, 182
Crescent planter, 151
Crests, 43, 91
Cruet, 45, 46, 50, 52, 54, 57, 59, 62, 64, 65, 82, 83, 95, 96, 97, 98, 104, 105, 110, 123, 141, 151, 152, 157, 160, 161, 169, 187
Crystal Overlay, 188
Custard glass, 99, 100, 106, 107, 108, 170, 174

D

Dahlia, 61, 70, 171, 172
Daisy & Button, 35, 54, 57, 58, 59, 79, 83, 106, 108, 111, 118, 121, 122, 123, 124, 125, 134, 148, 149, 152, 154, 155, 161, 162, 163, 164, 167, 168, 169, 170, 172, 173, 175, 176, 177, 178, 179, 180, 181, 182, 183, 184, 185, 186, 187
Daisy & Button Thumbprint Panel, 57, 121, 122, 123, 125, 134, 144, 148, 149, 156, 162, 163, 164, 175, 181
Daisy & Cube, 51, 132, 134, 147, 148, 150, 153, 162, 169, 174, 175, 183
Dark Blue Overlay, 85, 87, 89, 97
Decorations:
    "Acorn", 81, 82, 94
    Amber Daisy, 101
    Antique Golden Poppy, 101
    Bouquet, 89
    Brown Apple, 101, 103
    "Cherry", 94
    Daisy, 103
    "Dogwood", 83, 84
    "Floral", 83, 84, 95
    Forest etch, 150, 173
    Flower Band, 150, 174
    Gold Floral, 100
    Golden Rambling Rose, 174
    Grape, 88
    Green Floral, 88
    Grey Rose, 84, 101, 103
    Hibiscus, 136
    Holland Rose, 88, 101, 103, 182
    Mallow Rose, 90
    Mary Gregory, 105
    Moss Rose, 46, 54, 58, 81, 82, 83, 84, 91, 94, 99, 174, 188
    Mountain Poppy, 101, 174
    Paisley, 90
    Pansy, 107, 174
    Polynesian Rose, 90, 101
    Red Primrose, 67
    Rose, 103
    "Rose", 81, 82, 83, 84, 88, 94
    Rose Floral, 101
    Rose of Yesteryear, 58, 88, 90, 103, 182
    Rose Vine, 174
    Spring Bouquet, 84, 101, 103
    Spring Flowers, 89
    Strawberry, 100
    Sunset Rose, 174
    Toy Rose, 58, 88, 89
    Violet, 88
    Wild Rose, 88
    Woodrose, 102
    Yellow Rose, 90, 172
Deer & Pine Tree, 148, 150, 166
Diamond Panel Fruit, 147, 162
Diamond Quilted, 134, 147, 150, 152, 153, 177
Dolphin compote, 59, 153, 160, 169, 175
Double Wedding Ring, 126, 158, 170, 185
Dust Pan, 181

E

Embossed Bird, 86, 87
Embossed Rose, 51, 82, 84, 85, 87, 146, 159, 163, 168, 170, 172, 178, 182, 184, 189
Epergne, 91, 92
Eye Dot & Daisy, 63
Eye Winker, 127, 128, 129, 144, 145, 153, 163, 166, 182, 185, 188, 189

F

Ferdinand mustard jar, 40, 41
Fern, 43, 44, 45, 46, 47, 48, 49, 50, 52, 53, 54, 55, 57, 58, 59, 60, 62, 63, 64, 67, 82, 84, 94, 173, 182
Fish ashtray, 181, 183
Fish toothpick, 35, 183
Flat Iron candy box, 157, 169, 179, 187
Floral & Grape, 74
Flower frog, 110, 122
Fluted Vine (Vine), 50, 82, 83, 95, 97, 98, 104, 152, 169
Four Wheel Cart, 176, 177, 178
Frog toothpick, 168, 178, 183
Frosted Ribbon, 148, 150, 166

G

God & Home, 42, 73, 76, 77, 78, 79
Grape, 70, 72, 74, 76, 106, 107, 128, 157, 174
Grape & Cable, 72, 76
Grape & Daisy, 70, 106, 107, 174
Grape & Fruit, 70, 106, 108
Grape Vine Lattice, 74
Grasshopper, 150, 151
Green Overlay, 93
Gypsy Kettle, 123, 162

H

Hat, 123, 175
Herringbone, 134, 148, 149, 173, 175
Hi Button shoe, 182, 186
Hobnail, 38, 44, 51, 134, 148, 152, 153, 161, 162, 163, 169, 173, 175, 189
Holly, 106, 108
Honeycomb, 43, 44, 45, 46, 48, 49, 50, 51, 52, 53, 54, 82
Honeycomb pressed, 161
Hoot Owl relish, 187
Horn of Plenty, 134, 148, 149, 162
Horseshoe, 184

I

Inverted Dot, 149, 162
Inverted Strawberry, 169
Iris, 67
Ivy bowl, 57, 59, 118, 176

J

Jack in Pulpit vase, 93
Jersey Swirl, 59, 134, 144, 148, 160, 162, 163, 164, 185

K

Kings Crown, 147, 173
Kitten Slipper, 106, 108, 123, 169, 174

L

Lamp & lamp shades, 46, 51, 56, 60, 62, 64, 67, 80, 82, 83, 86, 91, 94, 96, 97, 98, 99, 132, 170, 172, 174, 179, 182, 184, 188, 189, 190
Lamp (epergne), 91
Lamp (fairy), 51, 80, 82, 83, 96, 97, 98, 170, 182, 184, 188, 189, 190
Lamp (hurricane), 62, 64
Lamp (miniature, toy), 51, 82, 83, 94, 132, 179, 188
Lamp (oil), 67, 91
Leaf ashtray, 178, 186
Light Blue Overlay, 97
Lion, 144, 148, 150
Lion bread plate, 144, 150
Lord's Supper bread plate, 165
Lustre, 46

M

Magnet & Grape, 135, 149
Maize, 85, 86, 87, 89, 182
Maple Leaf, 42, 66, 76, 77, 78, 136, 147, 149, 150, 152, 153, 166, 169, 175, 178
Match Holder, 123
Melon handled bonbon, 151
Milk glass, 38, 39, 40, 58, 67, 84, 85, 86, 87, 88, 90, 91, 93, 94, 101, 102, 103, 132, 136, 140, 147, 148, 152, 161, 162, 167, 168, 169, 172, 174, 175, 176, 177, 178, 182, 188
Mint Green Overlay, 89, 90
Mirror & Rose, 58, 163, 170, 174
Moon & Star, 57, 60, 91, 92, 109, 110, 111, 112, 113, 114, 115, 116, 117, 118, 121, 125, 132, 134, 144, 147, 151, 153, 158, 161, 162, 163, 164, 166, 167, 168, 175, 177, 179, 181, 185, 188, 189, 190
Morning Glory, 150, 151

N

New England Pineapple, 148

O

One-O-One, 148, 162
Opal Dot, 43, 44, 45, 48, 49, 50, 51, 52, 53, 54, 58, 182
Opal Eye Dot, 43, 44, 45, 49, 50, 51, 52, 54
Opal Hobnail, 44
Opal Lattice, 45, 49, 94
Opal Rib, 45, 50, 52, 54, 57, 59
Opal Swirl, 43, 44, 45, 48, 49, 50, 51, 52, 53, 54, 58, 81, 82, 182
Opalescent glass, 42, 43, 44, 45, 46, 47, 48, 49, 50, 51, 52, 53, 54, 55, 56, 57, 58, 59, 60, 61, 62, 63, 64, 65, 67, 81, 83, 84, 92, 94, 154, 160, 164, 170, 175, 182
"Open Edge" plate, 167
Open Lattice plate, 167

P

Panel Daisy, 121, 148
Panel Grape, 57, 89, 92, 129, 130, 131, 132, 133, 134, 144, 147, 148, 149, 153, 155, 156, 171, 175
Panel Sawtooth, 166, 184
Paperweight, 104, 175
Peach Blow, 46, 81, 82, 83, 84, 87, 91, 93, 94, 174, 188
Peacock, 79, 106, 108
Petticoat vase, 160
Pickle jar/caster, 49, 54, 58, 62, 64, 81, 82, 83, 87, 98, 122, 123, 124, 167, 170, 174, 182
Pink Overlay, 58, 85, 86, 87, 88, 89, 90, 182, 188
Plume, 94, 132, 147, 150, 166, 188
Pony, 71
Princess Feather, 159
Priscilla, 137, 138, 144, 158, 163, 185
Pump & Trough, 61, 70, 157, 163, 171, 182
Punch set, 129, 133, 155

Q

Queen Anne Slipper, 170, 182, 186
Quilt, 43, 45, 48, 49, 50

R

Rabbit toothpick, 183, 187
Rambler Rose, 70, 74
Rib, 43, 45, 48
Ribbed Palm Leaf, 158
Rooster toothpick, 183
Rose Bowl, 46, 62, 63, 64, 65, 72, 76, 81, 82, 83, 84, 85, 87, 89, 93, 95, 96, 97, 98, 104, 110, 122, 123, 137, 161, 163, 168, 170, 173, 175
Rose in Snow, 165
Rose Overlay, 85, 87, 188
Rose Sprig, 147, 150, 166
"Rustic" vase, 161

S

S, 35, 50, 106, 107, 112, 134, 138, 157, 161, 162, 169, 174, 185, 168, 175, 177, 179, 181, 185, 188, 189, 190
Salt dip, 109, 117, 123, 125, 134, 141, 142, 144, 161, 162, 165, 166, 169, 175, 180, 181, 183, 185, 186
Sandal, 168, 178
Sawtooth, 35, 121, 144, 185
Shell & Tassel, 148, 150, 166, 175, 181
Skillet, 184, 187
Slag glass, 35, 39, 40, 41, 42, 74, 104, 135, 171, 172
Sleigh, 124
Slipper, 79, 106, 108, 123, 169, 170, 174, 182, 186
Spatter glass, 104
Spooner, 65, 95, 98, 110, 117, 123, 136, 139, 140, 141, 142, 144, 169, 170
"Star" vase, 94
Stars & Stripes, 49, 52, 173, 175
Stipple Star, 134, 151, 153, 168, 185, 190
Stork, 190
Stork & Rushes, 68, 69, 79, 139, 140
Stove candy box, 157, 184, 187
Strawberry & Currant, 57, 59, 134, 148, 150, 157, 162, 163, 164, 169, 170, 182
Sugar shaker, 44, 49, 52, 54, 62, 64, 65, 86, 87, 95, 97, 98, 99, 100, 104, 116, 117, 141, 142, 152, 161, 169
Swan salt dip, 161, 169, 186
Sweetheart, 80, 134, 147, 153, 162, 183, 185, 190
Sweetheart Cherry, 74
Swirl, 43, 44, 45, 48, 50, 51
Syrup, 49, 52, 54, 62, 64, 65, 81, 82, 94, 173, 187

T

Thistle, 42, 75, 141, 144, 147, 151, 161, 165, 166, 172, 175, 186, 190
Thousand Eye, 147, 149, 165, 190
Three Face, 142, 144, 148, 161, 170, 181
Three Wheel Cart, 177, 187
Thumbprint, 43, 44, 45, 47, 48, 49, 50, 51, 52, 53, 54, 58, 82, 83, 84, 90, 147, 152, 173, 182
Toothpick, 35, 42, 57, 59, 61, 80, 106, 107, 117, 123, 125, 126, 134, 136, 138, 141, 142, 144, 162, 168, 170, 172, 174, 177, 178, 181, 182, 183, 185, 186, 187
Tree of Life, 145
Turkey toothpick, 182, 186
Twig, 106
Two Panel, 147, 175

V

Vaseline, 48, 49, 50, 51, 55, 57, 59, 60, 62, 63, 67, 117, 154, 164, 173, 175, 189, 190
Violin ashtray, 183, 186
Violin candy box, 156, 157, 187

W

Westward Ho, 143, 144, 148, 166
Wheat, 106, 107
Wheat & Barley, 159
Wildflower, 57, 146, 147, 148, 149, 164, 165, 172, 186
Wildrose, 128, 145, 146, 158, 159, 163, 170, 173, 182
Wildrose Satin (color), 96
Wild Rose (color), 151